Early Churches in South Dakota

Early Churches in South Dakota

A Lasting Legacy

ROBERT W. SEBESTA

with an essay by

ELIZABETH J. ALMLIE

SOUTH DAKOTA HISTORICAL SOCIETY PRESS Pierre

© 2018 by the South Dakota Historical Society Press.
All rights reserved. This book or portions thereof in any form whatsoever may not be reproduced without the expressed written approval of the South Dakota Historical Society Press, Pierre, S.Dak., 57501.

Early Churches in South Dakota is Volume Six in the Historical Preservation Series.

Library of Congress Cataloging-in-Publication data
Names: Sebesta, Robert W., author. | South Dakota State Historical Society.
Title: Early churches in South Dakota : a lasting legacy / by Robert W. Sebesta ; with an essay by Elizabeth J. Almlie.
Description: Pierre : South Dakota Historical Society Press, 2018. | Series: Volume Six in the Historical Preservation Series | Includes bibliographical references and index.
Identifiers: LCCN 2018022087 | ISBN 9781941813171 (pbk.)
Subjects: LCSH: Church buildings—South Dakota. | Church architecture—South Dakota. | South Dakota—Church history.
Classification: LCC NA5230.S8 S43 2018 | DDC 726.509783—dc23 LC record available at https://lccn.loc.gov/2018022087

The activity that is the subject of this book has been funded, in part, with financial assistance from the National Park Service through the South Dakota Historic Preservation Office (SHPO), a program that receives federal financial assistance from the National Park Service. Title VI of the Civil Rights Act of 1964, Section 504 of the Rehabilitation Act of 1973, the Americans with Disabilities Act of 1990, South Dakota law SDCL 20-13, the State of South Dakota, and the U.S. Department of the Interior prohibit discrimination on the basis of race, color, creed, religion, sex, disability, ancestry, or national origin. If you believe you have been discriminated against in any program, activity, or facility as described above, or if you desire more information, please write to Division of Human Rights (Labor & Management), South Dakota Department of Labor and Regulation, Kneip Building, 700 Governors Drive, Pierre, SD 57501-2291, or the Office of Equal Opportunity, National Park Service, 1201 I Street NW, Washington, D.C. 20005.

Printed in Canada

The paper in this book meets the guidelines for permanence and durability of the committee on Production Guidelines for Book Longevity of the Council on Library Resources.

Text and cover design by Rich Hendel and set by Kim Bryant

Frontispiece: Interior, Saint John's Episcopal Church, 1888 [9/9/2010]

Please visit our website at sdhspress.com

18 19 20 21 22 1 2 3 4 5

Contents

Preface

On a summer visit to my parents in Yankton in the early 2000s, I spent a couple hours in the Yankton Community Library. While there, I happened to find a copy of *History of Yankton County* and gave it a quick look. Almost immediately, I turned to the church section and was fascinated with the contribution of local people who had taken the time to research and write short histories of most of the churches in the county. The next day my parents, my two children, and I drove by a couple of the country churches I had read about in the county history. I have a long-standing interest in church architecture, having visited many of the great cathedrals of Europe. The churches in Yankton County clearly lacked the architectural grandeur of the cathedrals I had seen, but they were part of the prairie landscape, and the stories of how some of them came into existence proved fascinating to me. The tenacity and faith of the settlers who came to Dakota Territory after the 1860s were evident in the places of worship that continue to exist long after they and their ancestors were gone.

In June of 2005, after attending a family reunion near Kimball, I spent a few days finding and photographing some of the older churches in Brule County. I soon decided I would try to find all of the remaining churches in the state that were built before 1930. My goal was to photograph and find some history of each of them. At the time, I naively believed that the number of churches to document would not be too large.

Between 2005 and 2016, I drove to South Dakota from my home in Colorado twenty-five times, each time spending most of a week there, taking photographs and gathering historical information on old churches. Altogether, I logged at least fifty thousand miles and took more than fifteen hundred pictures, most with 35mm SLR cameras. In the last few years, I used digital cameras. I visited most of the towns in the state and drove on a great majority of its highways, including many miles of gravel roads. It is generous to call some of those roads graveled, for they were more often dirt. I visited all of the large libraries in the state and some of the smallest, the latter often open only a few hours a week. From the libraries, and also from some of the churches, I gathered historical information, but most helpful were the county history books. Most, but not all, of the sixty-six counties in South Dakota had produced history books, often in the year of their centennial, one hundred years after they were established.

In my travels, I found more than six hundred fifty churches built before 1930, most of them still being used at least occasionally. All but one of these is Christian; I found one Jewish synagogue, but no Islamic mosques or Buddhist temples that were built before 1930. Most of the churches had been remodeled or updated at least once since initial construction. Although many of the oldest churches were originally constructed of wood, built on foundations of stone, and roofed with wooden shingles, many now have aluminum siding, and most have either asphalt-shingle or steel roofs. Among the smaller churches, nearly all are built from wood. Most of the large churches in the larger towns, in contrast, are built from bricks or stone. The abundance of good building stone available in the east-central part of the state made it a natural construction material, especially in the region around Sioux Falls. This stone is quartzite, which was formed when sandstone was put under great heat and pressure. Because quartzite is highly resistant to weathering, buildings constructed with it tend to have long lifetimes, given adequate maintenance. Of course, even a

Pioneer Lutheran Church, 4 miles west, 2 miles north of White, Brookings County, built 1906, burned 2009 [5/20/2009]

hundred years ago, it was much cheaper to build a church with wood or brick than with cut stone, so there are not many quartzite churches.

The structure of this book is simple and chronological. The first chapter offers a brief history of the people, religions, and first churches in the southern half of Dakota Territory, including the oldest standing church in the state. The next six chapters correspond to the decades from the 1870s to the 1920s. Since my focus is on the church buildings, the historical context of life in what became South Dakota is necessarily brief, followed by short histories and photographs of a few of the more interesting churches, either historically or architecturally, built during the decade.

The last chapter includes pictures, names, locations, and years of construction of all of the remaining churches in South Dakota built before 1930 that I discovered in my research. I cannot claim that my list is comprehensive, but it offers a roadmap to most of the places of worship that still exist in each county, whether close to an interstate highway or hidden in a grove of trees along a winding country road. Within each county, the structures are in the order of their year of construction with brief notes.

While this book records the churches built between 1869 and 1930 that are still standing in South Dakota, each decade sees fewer churches remaining than the one before. Wind, fire, and neglect, among other things, take their toll on man-made structures such as church buildings. Let me give but one example. In the course of assembling this book, I selected Pioneer Lutheran Church of rural White, South Dakota, as one of the structures I wanted to highlight in the 1900s decade. A group of Danish immigrants had started the congregation that ultimately dedicated the building in 1906, and it had served the community into the twenty-first century. But in 2009, the church burned to the ground. In spite of such losses, South Dakota remains fortunate in its legacy of church structures, which the various communities do their best to preserve.

During my travels in South Dakota, I met and talked to many different people, who generously gave me directions to specific churches or offered information from their own familiarity with their historic landmarks. Among them were waitresses, shopkeepers, bartenders, librarians, police officers, and many farmers. I enjoyed immensely both seeing all of the nooks and crannies of the state and conversing with the locals. Preparing this book gave me a highly pleasurable series of adventures.

Robert W. Sebesta

NORTH
MONTANA
WYOMING
McIntosh
Standing Rock Reservation
GRAND RIVER
CORSON
Buffalo
Bison
HARDING
PERKINS
Timber Lake
MOREAU RIVER
DEWEY
Cheyenne River Reservation
Dupree
BUTTE
ZIEBACH
Belle Fourche
MEADE
BELLE FOURCHE RIVER
Deadwood
Sturgis
HAAKON
STANLEY
Ft. Pierre
LAWRENCE
Rapid City
Philip
BAD RIVER
PENNINGTON
CHEYENNE RIVER
JONES
BLACK HILLS
JACKSON
Kadoka
Murdo
Custer City
BADLANDS
CUSTER
WHITE RIVER
White Rive
Pine Ridge Reservation
MELLETTE
Hot Springs
OGLALA LAKOTA
BENNETT
Mission
TODD
FALL RIVER
Pine Ridge
Martin
Rosebud Reservation
MILES
0
25
50
75
100

KOTA
MCPHERSON
BROWN
Britton
ROBERTS
Sisseton
ound City
MPBELL
Leola
MARSHALL
EDMUNDS
elby
Aberdeen
ALWORTH
Ipswich
DAY
Webster
Milbank
POTTER
FAULK
GRANT
SPINK
CLARK
CODINGTON
ettysburg
Faulkton
Watertown
Redfield
Clark
HAMLIN
Clear Lake
HYDE
HAND
Hayti
ida
JAMES RIVER
DEUEL
KINGSBURY
BROOKINGS
Highmore
Miller
BEADLE
BIG SIOUX RIVER
Brookings
erre
Huron
De Smet
HUHES
MINNESOTA
Crow Creek Res.
Gann Valley
JERAULD
MINER
LAKE
Lower Brule Res.
Wessington Springs
Woonsocket
Howard
Madison
Flandreau
BUFFALO
MOODY
SANBORN
Kennebec
YMON
Chamberlain
HANSON
VERMILLION RIVER
MINNEHAHA
BRULE
Plankinton
Mitchell
Alexandria
MISSOURI RIVER
AURORA
DAVISON
Sioux Falls
IOWA
CHARLES MIX
DOUGLAS
Armour
HUTCHINSON
Parker
LINCOLN
Winner
TURNER
Lake Andes
Olivet
Canton
TRIPP
BON HOMME
YANKTON
Burke
Yankton Reservation
UNION
GREGORY
Tyndall
Yankton
CLAY
EBRASKA
Vermillion
Elk Point

Architecture and Inspiration

An Essay by Elizabeth J. Almlie

All buildings hold stories in their walls, but those of historic churches often reach further and deeper. Churches communicate religious feeling and philosophies, stories of belief and community, and traditions of craftsmanship and artistic expression. Few types of historic buildings embody the emotional charge that churches do, but even beyond the personal ties that church members and their families may have with a building, churches have played critical roles in the history of South Dakota. Churches and their leaders brought people together, supported social welfare, and set expectations for societal norms and moral behavior. They became gathering points in celebration or in crisis. Church buildings have become landmarks exhibiting their communities' investment in architectural design or local craftsmanship. South Dakota church buildings demonstrate a tremendous wealth of variety, from simple structures of small denominations, like the former African Methodist Episcopal (AME) Church in Yankton or the Harmony Friends Church near Wessington Springs, to finely detailed structures of larger denominations, like Saint Joseph's Cathedral of the Catholic Diocese in Sioux Falls or First Congregational (now Faith Temple) Church in Rapid City.

Some of the first Euro-Americans to enter this territory were missionaries, traveling with fur traders or venturing on their own expeditions, to teach and minister to fellow newcomers and the Dakota and Lakota tribes ocupying these lands. Relationships between tribes and missionaries varied, but most had significant impacts on Sioux life in cultural practices, social organization, education, and political power, both within tribes and with the United States government. Sent to the tribes by their denominations or, later, to assigned reservations with federal authority, missionaries often started by traveling place to place, but they eventually built churches and missions where tribal members worshiped or trained as ministers, took part in and taught at schools, attended social gatherings, cheered on sports teams, and received medical advice and care from nurses.

Though the official goals of missions typically included conversion and Americanization, tribal members also used local missions to push back against assimilation and eventually to recapture traditional family relationships, languages, and cultural practices. For instance, the Catholic missions held annual Indian Congress events at various locations each year, which provided time for extended families to reconnect in the way that traditional summer gatherings once had. Dakota Sioux women of the First Presbyterian Church near Flandreau regularly traveled some distance to meet together to quilt and work on other projects that would raise funds for their church and wider Presbyterian mission efforts.[1]

Although mission churches were often simple structures built with available materials like the log church (1877) at the Brown Earth colony, they became more elaborate over time. Some of the early churches, such as the First Presbyterian Church/Whakapapa's Okadiciye (1873) near Flandreau and the Ascension/Iyakaptapi Church (1870) near Ortley, were wood-frame structures with tall center steeples of the Prairie Gothic–type common across the plains. Later in the twentieth century, some reservation missions built exquisite churches, often with elements constructed or added by church members or students. The Romanesque-styled Saint Charles Borromeo Church (1919) at Saint Francis on the

Rosebud Indian Reservation and the Gothic-styled Saint Paul's Church (1942) at Marty on the Yankton Indian Reservation are both Catholic mission churches that feature high architectural design with detailed interior decorative painting, incorporating a blend of religious iconography and traditional styles. A smaller building, also architect designed, was the Holy Spirit Chapel (1923), built with local stone near Timber Lake on the Standing Rock Indian Reservation.

As larger numbers of Euro-Americans began to arrive and lay out farms and settlements, churches became critical elements of the changing landscape. For homesteaders, farmers, and townbuilders, churches provided a desired sense of normality, stability, and comfort in the midst of their dreams and uncertainties and through cycles of boom and bust. Churches could facilitate relationships between new neighbors and create a connection with the family and communities they had left behind. Once congregations were large and stable enough to build a house of worship, they seemed to believe "that a church inspired by architecture of the old country could also nurture connections across oceans, continents, and time with their past homes."[2] Churches followed settlement and immigration across the state, from Czech churches in Bon Homme County, German Mennonite churches around Freeman, Reformed churches in Dutch communities around Platte, to Finnish churches in farm communities near Frederick and in the mining town of Lead.

Churches also had historical impacts beyond their buildings. Churches and church leaders often established schools (from day schools to colleges), founded and staffed hospitals, and took active roles in the civic life of their communities. Reverend Joseph Ward, a Congregational minister in Yankton, not only founded First Congregational Church in Yankton but also Yankton College, and he was active in the early movement for statehood in the 1880s. In 1885, in the Wessington Springs area, leaders of the Harmony Friends Church, including S. F. and Abbie Huntley and Rhoda Marshall, were also leaders in local temperance and suffrage movements. In the 1930s, in the midst of the Great Depression, Sister Jerome Schmitt successfully led efforts to turn the Catholic high school academy in Yankton into a junior college, which opened in 1936. Sister Jerome's tenure as founding president of Mount Marty College lasted until 1957. During World War II, Saint John's Baptist Church in Sioux Falls provided space in their building for the first United Service Organizations (USO) for black soldiers stationed at the Army Air Force Radio Technical Training School in town until they could erect a building of their own.[3]

The history of church architecture in South Dakota is classified into several distinct trends in building types, called "generations," although the timing between types varied greatly for each congregation, depending on many factors. Some congregations dissolved before outgrowing their first small churches, while others organized late enough that their first building was architect designed. First-generation churches were typically simple buildings constructed with available local materials such as sod, logs, or stone. As soon as resources became available from sawmills, brickyards, and rail-connected lumberyards, carpenters and stonemasons used milled lumber and stone for slightly larger or more elaborate but still simply laid out transitional generation churches. Second-generation churches were often built when congregations became more established with a larger membership. These buildings employed more substantial and expensive materials like brick or dressed stone and used designs from professional architects. Rural congregations often built second or third buildings near the site of their first church unless their population relocated. Urban churches sometimes rebuilt or expanded their first buildings near the city core or built larger facilities in developing residential or commercial areas.

Denomination and ethnicity also affected the location of churches in urban settings. Many Catholic churches sought visibility through height, either in building type or in topography. Mainline Protestant churches were often first established in the center of the city, while smaller German, Swedish, and other ethnic-specific denominations were often built in the second ring of development outside downtown, nearer to where their members lived and where land prices were likely to be more affordable.

A majority of architecturally elaborate churches have used historicist styles in either European or American traditions. Across denominations, Gothic Revival in particular was often considered proper architecture for churches, in the same way that many thought Classical designs were proper for civic and governmental buildings. Medieval English and French churches had inspired the Gothic Revival style. Designs drew the eye vertically and incorporated additional light for the sanctuary by using taller windows and stained glass. Gothic Revival churches often feature pointed "lancet" arches in windows and doors, tall steeples or bell towers, buttresses to support lighter sidewalls, and may incorporate asymmetry in the building plan or features. In South Dakota, they varied greatly from simple wood-frame buildings like Saint Lawrence O'Toole Catholic Church (1879) in Central City to the "Carpenter Gothic" style of the Groton Episcopal Church (1884) with board-and-batten wood siding. Examples of larger stone buildings with elaborate Gothic tracery in stained-glass windows include the Sacred Heart Catholic Church (1930) in Aberdeen and the Bishop Marty Chapel (1950) in Yankton.

Romanesque-style churches, derived from earlier medieval European traditions, may share some characteristics with the Gothic Revival style but often have smaller windows, rounded arches, and draw from classical motifs. Most common in South Dakota for Catholic churches, examples include Saint Peter's Catholic Church (1891) in Jefferson, Saint Mary's Church of the Immaculate Conception (1902) in Rapid City, Saint Joseph's Cathedral (1919) in Sioux Falls, and Saint Charles Borromeo Catholic Church (1919) in Saint Francis. New York architect H. H. Richardson is credited with inspiring a popular American derivation of the Romanesque style in the late-nineteenth century. Richardsonian Romanesque buildings use rounded arches but have exaggerated design compositions with more variation, asymmetry, and heavier masonry. South Dakota examples were often built with local quarried stone, including First Baptist Church (1889) in Vermillion, the former Presbyterian Church (1891) in Hot Springs, the Canton Lutheran Church (1908), and First United Methodist (1907) in Mitchell.

Less common, Classical-styled churches, such as the First Presbyterian and First Congregational churches in Huron or First Congregational Church in Rapid City, used elements of Greek classical architecture, including symmetrical designs with triangular pediments and classical columns. Denominations with "Yankee" roots in New England often selected Colonial Revival designs, as seen in the First Congregational Church in Watertown, First Baptist Church in Viborg, and the Free Methodist Evangelical Church in Yankton. Margaret Wellington based her ideas for the design of her church, the First Congregational Church (1929) in Vermillion, on her memories of the Congregational churches she knew growing up in Massachusetts.[4]

Other architectural styles are seen in a select number of early South Dakota churches as well:

Tudor Revival designs with prominent gables and exposed timbers in the walls; Mission Revival or Spanish Colonial designs with baroque parapets, stucco, or tile roofs; and Prairie School designs with boxy massing and horizontal bands across the walls or rows of windows.

Basic church building plans in South Dakota typically included three sections: the narthex, where the congregation entered the building; the nave of the sanctuary, where the congregation sat for services; and the chancel, where the altar was located. The simplest naves include two sections of pews or other seating with a center aisle. Designs to achieve a greater capacity and complexity might include additional sections of seating in the sanctuary and the balcony, choir lofts, or the use of curved or polygonal layouts. Basilica-plan churches derived from medieval European church layouts, which created a cruciform, or cross, in the shape of the church itself, with a long nave and transepts to either side before the chancel. Basilica-plan churches often have side aisles in the nave with structural columns and arches, and many have round or polygonal apses behind the chancel for the altar. Significant examples of the basilica plan in Catholic churches include Saint Bernard/Saint Anthony of Padua in Hoven, Saint Mary's in Salem, Saint Peter's in Jefferson, and Saint Charles Borromeo at the Saint Francis Mission. Less common "non-ritual" plans include the audience-hall plan, with seating arranged like an auditorium around the chancel, and the Akron plan, with adjoining classrooms that could be set off from the sanctuary with sliding or folding doors to accommodate the newly popular Sunday schools. One example of the Akron plan in South Dakota is the Presbyterian Church in Groton, which was designed with a polygonal sanctuary and a space on the west end of the sanctuary that can be divided into a central gathering space and smaller classrooms for a Sunday school program. Many churches added basements or additional wings to the building for classroom spaces, as well as offices and fellowship halls, during the twentieth century, when changing practices or improved resources made them desirable.

For many churches, members worked together to plan and build the church buildings. At the Garfield Lutheran Church near Bryant, the Ladies' Aid Society took a leading role in fundraising for a building, and when the five men who formed the building committee had a plan ready, members brought in stones from their fields for the foundation and two of the men on the committee oversaw the carpentry work to build the wood-frame structure. At Hoven, the immense "Cathedral on the Prairie" was only possible because many members contributed labor, in addition to funding, to erect the brick church. In 1983, members again contributed labor to complete a major restoration of the historic church.

When members participated in church design, construction, and furnishing, the buildings often reflected folk or vernacular traditions of diverse backgrounds and ethnicities. Many Scandinavian churches had prominent or intricate woodwork, while Catholic churches of German, Czech, or Irish descent used distinctive decoration, motifs, or iconography. Others, like Hutterite, Society of Friends, and smaller Baptist churches have much simpler, minimally ornamented sanctuaries that reflect their denominational beliefs.

Of the many South Dakota architects who designed churches, there are several who stand out. Some worked more often within particular denominations; others with particular communities. Joseph Schwarz was a German Catholic architect in Sioux Falls who found consistent work from the Catholic diocese. He and his firm, which included his son Joseph Schwarz, Jr., designed at least thirty-four churches between

1896 and 1926, twenty-six of which were for the Roman Catholic Church. Schwarz also designed several parochial schools and parish residences, as well as many other types of buildings.

Wallace L. Dow of Sioux Falls is arguably the best-recognized South Dakota architect of the nineteenth century. Like Schwarz, he did a wide variety of work that included at least seven churches of various denominations built between 1882 and 1903. In the early twentieth century, other South Dakota architects designed several churches each, including George Issenhuth of Huron, Maurice Hockman of Watertown, John Chapman of Sioux Falls, and George Fossum of Aberdeen. Several churches also hired architects or bought plans from architects outside the state. Designs by Milwaukee architect Anton Dohmen were used for eight Catholic churches in South Dakota between 1903 and 1918. Six Protestant churches in northeastern South Dakota used designs from Minneapolis architect Harry W. Jones between 1914 and 1921, and three Lutheran churches—one near Richland in Union County, one in Watertown, and one in Madison—chose nearly identical plans from Minneapolis architect Peter O. Moe.[5] These architectural legacies are embodied in South Dakota churches.

In light of the immense historical and architectural legacy connected to our churches, the continued use and maintenance of these buildings present opportunities and challenges for keeping them as vital elements of South Dakota communities today. At many points, members and community residents have made decisions that have either preserved these connections to our history or left them to erode over time. Maintenance and repair projects take resources that might not be available. Locating craftspeople with the background to maintain and make repairs to the intricate or specialized features of historic church buildings can also be difficult.

Changing demographics can create challenges as well. Some congregations outgrow their buildings and move on to new structures. Some design extensive renovations or additions that can have a big impact on the character of the historic building. In cases, alterations can be designed without obscuring the historic building, but other changes erase or mask distinctive materials, craftsmanship, or functional spaces. Other congregations face dwindling membership and may sell their buildings to new owners. If still in compatible use, changes might be slight, but it can be difficult to reuse a church building with sensitivity while adapting special use spaces like sanctuaries for another purpose. When there is no new occupant, some church buildings have suffered from complete abandonment. Others, such as the Oahe Chapel in Pierre, Garfield Lutheran near Bryant, the old Vangen Lutheran Church near Mission Hill, Harmony Friends Church, Brown Earth Presbyterian Church, and the Yankton AME Church, have been vacant or sparsely used but have found dedicated caretakers who put valuable time and resources into maintaining the current buildings and accommodating the occasional service, wedding, or cultural event. Former members and their descendants often highly treasure such stewardship.

One opportunity for documenting and recognizing these church buildings and their histories is through the National Register of Historic Places. Churches are typically not eligible for the National Register based solely on their status as a church, but they might be eligible for their association with significant events or trends or for their architectural significance. Eligibility also depends on the "historic integrity" of the surviving physical characteristics of the building and the impact of any alterations. Successful National Register nominations include full descriptions of the buildings, as well as histories associated with the building, which become part of the national historical record. Buildings listed in the National Register, either as an individual building or as a contributing part of a historic district group of buildings, may be eligible for grants from preservation agencies and organizations. Churches in South Dakota have used both the Deadwood Fund Grant from the South Dakota State Historical Society and the Outside-of-Deadwood Grant from the City of Deadwood. There are also limited national grant opportunities from organizations like the National Trust for Historic Preservation or from private groups or foundations. The preservation of South Dakota's historic church buildings gives us an incredible legacy of stories critical to our state history and of workmanship and artistry that enriches our communities.

NOTES

1. First Presbyterian Church and Cemetery/Wakpaipaksan Okadiciye, Flandreau, Moody County, National Register of Historic Places (NRHP) Nomination (July 2017), National Register Information Service (NRIS) #SG100001402, National Park Service, nps.gov/nr/.

2. Megan Eades, *Churches in South Dakota*, South Dakota State Historic Preservation Office Context Document (Pierre, 2002), p. 5.

3. Harmony Friends Church, Wessington Springs vicinity, Jerauld County, NRHP Nomination (Sept. 2015), NRIS #15000565, nps.gov/nr/; *Yankton Press & Dakotan*, 29 Sept. 2014; Sara L. Bernson and Robert J. Eggers, "Black People in South Dakota History," *South Dakota History* 7 (Fall 1977): 262–63.

4. Edward C. Ehrensperger, *A Little Church on the Prairie: A Brief History of the United Church of Christ in Vermillion, South Dakota, formerly known as the First Congregational Church* (Vermillion, S.Dak.: n.p., 1970), p. 24.

5. Architect Files, South Dakota State Historic Preservation Office, Pierre. *See* David Erpestad and David Wood, *Building South Dakota: A Historical Survey of the State's Architecture to 1945*, Historical Preservation Series, no. 1 (Pierre: South Dakota Historical Society Press, 1997), pp. 59–75.

1 : Before 1870

The Oldest Standing Church in South Dakota

By 1870, the largest group of people inhabiting the southern half of Dakota Territory were the Sioux, comprised of four major subtribes: the Yanktons, the Yanktonais, the Santees, and the Tetons. The Yanktons and Yanktonais occupied the southeastern part of what became South Dakota, while the Tetons (Oglala, Brûlé, Two Kettle, Sans Arc, Blackfoot, Hunkpapa, and Minneconjou) occupied much of the rest. Before the white settlers arrived, the Santees lived in the southwestern half of what is now Minnesota. The Sioux referred to themselves as Dakotas, Nakotas, or Lakotas, reflecting dialects of the same base language that they all spoke. The first non-Indian people to venture into the area were trappers and others involved in the fur trade. Most of them were French and therefore Catholics. The first Catholic priest to travel through the fur-trade areas along the Missouri River was a Belgian, Father Pierre-Jean DeSmet, who first arrived in Saint Louis in 1820. In 1839, he visited the Indians who lived near where the Vermillion River empties into the Missouri (near the present-day town of Vermillion). He ministered to the French fur traders and converted many Lakota people as a circuit-riding priest, meaning he did not build churches or establish permanent congregations.[1]

Father De Smet and other French Catholic missionaries who worked with the Sioux as early as the late seventeenth century were not the only Euro-Americans to influence the Indians on the Northern Great Plains.[2] The first Protestant ministers to arrive were Presbyterians, who began working with Santees, or Dakota Indians, in the Minnesota River Valley in 1835. Even though the Sioux and other American Indians had their own spirituality and related customs, the missionaries saw conversion and education as the most effective way to help the Indians and assimilate them into agricultural life on the Plains. By the 1870s, the Presbyterian church had established the Greenwood Mission and day school on the Yankton Indian Reservation near the present-day town of Pickstown in Charles Mix County and another at the Oahe Mission near Fort Pierre. The Catholic church established churches and boarding schools on the Rosebud Indian Reservation in 1885 and on the Pine Ridge Indian Reservation in 1887. Episcopalians began working with the Sioux Indians in the 1860s and, by the early 1870s, had established churches and both boarding and day schools on three reservations: the Yankton, the Crow Creek, and the Cheyenne River.[3] The Methodist church sent clergy into the area to minister to the white settlers but did not try to Christianize the Indians.

Among the early non-Indian settlers of Dakota Territory was a remarkable homogeneity of organized religions. There were essentially no Jews, Muslims, Hindis, or Buddhists; nearly all of the early settlers who belonged to a religious organization were Christians. The most common Protestant denominations aligned with the religious affiliations in the newcomers' countries of origin. Because many of the early immigrants were from northern Europe, primarily Germany and the Scandinavian countries where the Lutheran church predominated, those immigrants naturally founded Lutheran congregations when they arrived in the United States. Religious denominations that originated in Great Britain were also common, among them Methodists, Episcopalians, Presbyterians, Baptists, and Congregationalists. In 1839, the Episcopalians and Methodists joined together to create a new Methodist-Episcopalian (ME) denomination,

An early sod church in South Dakota, 1895. *South Dakota State Historical Society, Digital Archives*

although some congregations chose to retain their separate and individual affiliation. Because there were Catholics in all of the European countries from which settlers came, they united to create many Catholic congregations.

Throughout the state, the earliest church buildings were built from sod, which was the construction material for many of the earliest houses and barns. The use of sod was necessary because of the scarcity of trees on the prairie. As transportation improved in a newly settled area, lumber was imported for the construction of wood-frame houses, barns, and churches. Only later and, for the most part, only in larger towns were churches constructed of either brick or stone. The majority of early churches were small, often just a single room, with a cathedral ceiling and a steeple attached to the front.

With transportation limited to walking and riding horseback or in a horse-drawn carriage or sled, members of the congregations needed churches they could reach on a Sunday morning. This reality led to the building of a large number of country churches, many of which have disappeared since the 1930s as rural populations diminished. Small wood-frame churches were also vulnerable to damage from the strong thunderstorm downdrafts and tornadoes that frequent the Northern Plains.

Presbyterian minister Charles D. Martin built the first church in what became South Dakota. Reverend Martin ventured into the area between the Big Sioux and Missouri rivers in 1859. In August 1860, his church in Vermillion emerged out of large cottonwood logs taken from abundant trees near the Missouri River along the Nebraska border. The small building had a log and earthen roof that leaked when it rained. The dirt that the rainwater brought with it made the church a far from ideal place to conduct religious services, at least when it poured. Perhaps because of its deficiencies, the church was torn down in 1862. In 1865, Episcopal priest Father Melancthon Hoyt built the first church in Yankton. During his career in the area, Father Hoyt organized more than fifty parishes and oversaw the building of seventeen churches.[4]

Norwegian immigrants began to appear in the southeastern part of what became Dakota Territory in 1859. In 1861, a theology student, Abraham Jacobson, came with settlers from Iowa and held services in several homes in the area. Jacobson did not stay long, but the Lutherans continued to hold religious meetings in homes. They also sought a pastor to visit them twice a year to minister to their religious needs. In early October 1864, a Lutheran pastor, Rev. J. Krohn, arrived in southeast Dakota Territory from Chicago to answer that need. After a service he held in a home near Vermillion on 8 October, Reverend Krohn and those in attendance organized the Norwegian Evangelical Lutheran Congregation in Dakota Territory. It included all Norwegian Lutherans in Union, Clay, and Yankton

Old Vangen Lutheran Church, Mission Hill, Yankton County, 1869 [5/23/2012]

counties. Reverend Krohn returned to the parish the following year.

After being called by the congregation, Rev. Emil Christenson arrived in 1867 to become the resident Lutheran pastor. The Norwegian Evangelical Lutheran Congregation had three districts: in the east, Brule Creek (in Union County); in the west, Vangen (in Yankton County); and in the middle, Bergen (in Clay County). Brule Creek recruited a second pastor, while Reverend Christenson served the other two districts until 1876. Services were held in homes and schools in the first few years, but in 1869, Guro Leverson donated land for a church and small cemetery one mile east of the town of Mission Hill, a few miles east of Yankton.

That church, built in 1869, was the first Lutheran church in Dakota Territory. Now called Old Vangen Lutheran, it was constructed largely from materials hauled from Sioux City in wagons pulled by oxen. The church was lit with kerosene lamps and heated with a pot-bellied stove in a room behind the altar. In 1918, a larger Vangen Lutheran Church was completed in Mission Hill, and the congregation moved to the new structure. At the time of the move, the congregation shifted from worshiping in Norwegian to English. The Old Vangen Lutheran has been preserved, along with some of its original contents, including its pulpit and baptismal font. It is the oldest standing church in South Dakota.[5]

NOTES

1. Herbert S. Schell, *History of South Dakota*, 4th ed., rev. John E. Miller (Pierre: South Dakota Historical Society Press, 2004), pp. 63–64.

2. Father De Smet was actively involved in bringing Indian leaders to a meeting that resulted in the Fort Laramie Treaty of 1851, as well as convincing Sitting Bull to join Red Cloud and other chiefs in the negotiations of the Laramie Treaty of 1868. *See* Paul VanDevelder, *Savages and Scoundrels: The Untold Story of America's Road to Empire through Indian Territory* (New Haven, Conn.: Yale University Press, 2009), pp. 195–96, 223.

3. Schell, *History of South Dakota*, p. 307.

4. George W. Kingsbury, *History of Dakota Territory*, vol. 1 (Chicago: S. J. Clarke Co., 1915), pp. 128–29, 214–15.

5. Yankton County Historical Society, *History of Yankton County, South Dakota* (Dallas, Tex.: Curtis Media Corp., 1987), pp. 146–47.

2 : The 1870s

Following the tumultuous decade of the 1860s, with its conflicts between whites and Indians and the United States Army, most of the American Indians living in Dakota Territory were on reservations in the western part of the area, and the eastern portion of the land was open for white settlement. By 1870, approximately ten thousand whites lived in the southern half of Dakota Territory, mostly in the southeast. The population increased by some 735 percent during the decade, from 11,776 people in 1870 to 98,268 in 1880. Land claim statistics also give evidence of rapid settlement. In 1877, land claims totaled 163,739 acres; in 1878, they represented 941,800 acres; and by 1879, land claims covered 1,075,560 acres. The Dakota Southern Railroad from Sioux City, Iowa, was extended to Yankton in 1873, which facilitated the settling of southeastern Dakota. During the decade of the 1870s, a significant number of churches were built, eleven of which still stand.[1]

Many of those who immigrated to Dakota Territory in the early 1870s came from Scandinavia. In the lower Big Sioux River Valley, they were mostly Norwegians. In Turner County, with settlement initially centered in Daneville, the immigrants came from Denmark. In western Yankton County and in Bon Homme County, initially around Lakeport and later around Tabor, the immigrants came from Bohemia.[2] One of the biggest ethnic groups to settle in Dakota Territory during the Great Dakota Boom (1878–1885) came from Russia, but they were people with German roots and ancestry. Between 1700 and 1770, Russia had encouraged German immigrants to settle in its southern region, allowing them to maintain their German culture and language and exempting them from military conscription. Many Mennonites and Hutterites, who were pacifists, immigrated to Russia to escape persecution in Germany. In 1871, however, the Russian government changed its policy and gave the immigrant Germans a decade to adopt the Russian culture and language or leave. Many chose to move to North America. About five hundred Lutheran German-Russians settled in Yankton County in 1873. About a thousand Mennonites settled in Turner County in 1874. Also in 1874, forty German-Russian families arrived in Bon Homme County and established the first Hutterite colony there. During the next fifty years, sixteen more Hutterite colonies were created in the southern half of Dakota Territory, all but the first in the areas of the lower James and Vermillion river valleys. The Hutterites lived in religious communes, with all property and goods owned by the commune.[3]

Meanwhile, although the Fort Laramie Treaty of 1868 had created the Great Sioux Reservation that included all of western South Dakota, the western third of the reservation, which contained the Black Hills, continued to attract attention because of reports of gold deposits there. Lieutenant Colonel George Armstrong Custer had led an expedition into the region from Fort Abraham Lincoln near Bismarck to scout locations for a fort. Although prospecting was not part of their mission, expedition members found gold and it soon became public knowledge, greatly increasing the number of prospectors who tried to enter the Black Hills and leading to a sequence of events that culminated in the Battle of the Little Big Horn near present-day Hardin, Montana. The results of this encounter had profound effects on the Sioux and their relationship with the army and the white settlers. Congress quickly dropped its negotiations with the Sioux to allow prospectors and other settlers into the Black Hills. Instead, they simply let it be known that the area would

First Presbyterian Church, Flandreau, Moody County, 1873 [8/9/2006]

no longer be protected from white intruders. By then, however, more than ten thousand white gold seekers already occupied the area illegally. The Sioux Agreement of 1877 officially opened the area for white settlement,[4] and settlers and town builders followed.

FIRST PRESBYTERIAN CHURCH, Flandreau, 1873

In 1862, conflict between the United States government and the Dakotas, or Santees, in Minnesota erupted in what is now called the Dakota War of 1862.[5] Following the war, government officials held the Santees they arrested for trial in a prison in Mankato, Minnesota, while their families were sent to Fort Snelling. The Santee families were moved several times, including a forced stay at the Crow Creek Indian Reservation in Dakota Territory. Eventually, they were moved to the Niobrara Indian Reservation (later named the Santee Indian Reservation) in northern Nebraska. After military trials ended with the execution of thirty-nine warriors in Mankato, the remaining prisoners were eventually relocated to Niobrara, where they were reunited with their families after nearly three years of separation. On 21 July 1866, under the guidance of Rev. John P. Williamson, 382 Indians, including 225 who had been moved from Crow Creek, formed the Pilgrim Presbyterian Church.[6] Reverend Williamson had been working with the Santee prisoners during their captivity in Minnesota.

For the next two years, the Santees were uncertain of their future. The government had moved their agency several times, and they feared they would be relocated to a more arid place. Some of the leaders were invited to participate in the negotiations of the Laramie Treaty of 1868, which they did. The treaty allowed any Indian who did not receive a tract of land on a reservation to homestead on public lands, provided they relinquished their tribal rights to government annuities. Successful homesteaders would be granted citizenship. Given the uncertainty of their lives, some Dakotas began to consider leaving the reservation and seeking homesteads. In October of 1868, several Santee families went north to hunt and to search for a suitable place for homesteading. They found such a place on a bend in the Big Sioux River, near the present-day town of Flandreau in Moody County. It was a fertile valley with trees along the river and plentiful game. In the last week of February 1869, one to two dozen Santee families, along with Reverend Williamson, began building log houses there. Because they had few horses, many of these travelers walked the one hundred and thirty miles from Niobrara to the "bend in the river." During the difficult journey, they encountered a blinding Northern Great Plains blizzard and received rations from Fort Dakota, which was near the present site of Sioux Falls. On 3 October, forty-seven inhabitants of the new Santee village met and formed the Church at the River Bend, or River Bend Church.

In June of 1870, twenty-five Santee men signed a document in Yankton that forfeited their rights to annuities from the government and stated their desire to homestead on public land. During the summer of 1871, the Santee began to build a log meeting house to be used as a church. On 1 August, J. W. Edwards of Marquette, Michigan, contributed five hundred dollars for the construction of a church, followed by a bequest from the Second Presbyterian Church of Springfield, Ohio, for another two hundred dollars. The log construction was immediately halted, and plans were made to build a wood-frame meeting house. The Santees purchased lumber from Windom, Minnesota, eighty miles east of the new settlement, and hauled it by wagon to their building site.

The original frame meeting house soon became inadequate as more and more Santee people moved from Nebraska to the Bend in the River community. A new, larger church was a necessity. In August of 1873, Reverend Williamson visited the new community from the Yankton reservation and offered to pay for some of the lumber to build a new church. The government bought the original meeting house for one thousand dollars and used it as a day school, first for Indian children and later for both Indian and white children. After its restoration in 1992, this meeting house stands today in the Moody County Museum grounds about six miles from its original location.

For the new church, the Santees purchased the lumber in Winona, in southeast Minnesota. Because of a lack of soft wood around Winona, white pine logs were shipped from Wisconsin and Minnesota to the lumber mill in Winona. Railroad cars carried the lumber to Marshall, Minnesota, where it was unloaded to oxen-pulled wagons, which hauled it the eighty miles to the church's building site, a journey that took several days.

The church design was for a twenty-four-by-fifty-foot building, with eight arched top windows, wainscoting, pine panels for the walls and ceiling, and a tall steeple. Francis and Anne Hawley purchased a fifteen-acre plot on a hill overlooking the river valley for fifteen dollars, and a local carpenter, P. A. Vannice, who was also the government schoolteacher, was hired to build the church. Men of the congregation helped. They used concrete, quartzite, and fieldstone to build the foundation. Church members donated $175 for a four-hundred pound bell for the church, made in Troy, New York.

This structure is the oldest continuously used church in South Dakota. During the early years of the First Presbyterian Church, it was used by the non-Indian Second Presbyterian, Methodist, and Baptist congregations until they built their own churches. In 2003, the church was completely restored, including replacement of the steeple. One of the major accomplishments of this church congregation was the establishment of the first Indian school in Flandreau in 1879.[7]

ASCENSION PRESBYTERIAN CHURCH, rural Peever, 1874

Ascension Presbyterian Church is the oldest church in both Roberts County and the northeast part of what became South Dakota. The congregation was formed in 1868 with forty-five members who built a frame church six years later in 1874. The Ascension Presbyterian Church is located five miles south and four miles west of the small town of Peever in Spring Grove Township.

Ascension Presbyterian Church, rural Peever, Roberts County, 1874 [7/17/2007]

Brown Earth Presbyterian Church, rural Stockholm, Grant County, 1877 [7/16/2007]

The town, with a 2010 population of 168, is about eight miles west of the Minnesota border and within the Lake Traverse Indian Reservation. The Lake Traverse Treaty of 1867 created the reservation, which straddles present-day South Dakota and North Dakota. It was originally formed to be a home for parts of the Santee tribe, specifically the Sisseton and Wahpeton subtribes. Indian churches on reservations at that time were given forty acres of land.

The congregation, organized in 1868, did not name the church solely for the ascension of Christ during the first Holy Week. Instead, the church was built in a hilly area, and many members had to ascend at least one hill to attend services. The second minister of the church, Rev. John B. Renville, who was ordained in 1865, was the first Santee Indian to become an ordained Presbyterian minister. He served the church for thirty-three years, from 1870 until his death in 1903. The church is still in regular use.[8]

BROWN EARTH PRESBYTERIAN CHURCH, rural Stockholm, 1877

Not long after the establishment of the Lake Traverse Indian Reservation, the residents split into two opposing groups: the "church party," members of which had converted to Christianity, and the "scout party," whose members had served as scouts for the army in the Dakota War of 1862. The Homestead Act had been extended to Indians, providing that they relinquish their tribal rights to annuities. This factor, among others, induced about twenty-five families of the "church party" to leave the Lake Traverse Indian Reservation and establish a new settlement they named Brown Earth. In 1877, they built a Presbyterian church there, not surprisingly named the Brown Earth Church. The structure is located two miles north and two miles east of the small town of Stockholm (with a 2010 population of 108), in southwest Grant County.[9]

Built from oak logs of local origin, the church is sometimes called the Old Indian Church. Although likely begun with great expectations,

Oahe Chapel, rural Pierre, Hughes County, 1877
[5/25/2010]

the settlement soon declined. In 1886, there were thirty-three families in the settlement, but only a dozen had received homesteads. When the Dawes Act in 1887 allotted each Indian head of a family the same amount of land on the reservation that white settlers were given on other government land, some of the people at Brown Earth chose to return to their original homes in Minnesota. Prior to this time, all reservation lands were owned by Indian tribes collectively rather than by individuals. The Brown Earth Church was abandoned after 1886.

Six years later, the Elim Covenant of Stockholm, South Dakota, bought the abandoned building; in 1901, they sold it to the Christian Church at Strandburg. In the late 1920s, American Legion Post No. 171 in Stockholm and Strandburg took responsibility for maintaining the building. They installed a concrete floor and replaced some of the original logs. The Old Settlers Society and Grant County Historical Association purchased the church in 1945, and in the next decade, the Peppy Pals 4-H Club planted trees near the structure. Since then, it has been the site of school and county picnics and an occasional worship service.

OAHE CHAPEL, rural Pierre, 1877

Congregational minister Rev. Thomas L. Riggs and his first wife, Cornelia Foster Riggs, established the Oahe Mission in 1874 to serve the Sioux Indians in what later became central South Dakota. The mission was located on the east bank of the Missouri River, about five miles upriver from Pierre at the former site of an Arikara village named Ti Tanke Ohe. The mission adopted the name, although it was soon shortened to Oahe. The first building at the mission was a log house, but by 1877, it had become too small to use as a meeting house. The Lakotas in the vicinity of the mission helped Reverend Riggs build the Oahe Chapel, using lumber brought by steamboat from Sioux City.

Like many such structures, the chapel served as both church and school in its first few years before the mission opened the Oahe Industrial School for Indian boys in 1883 and a second boarding school for Indian girls in the 1890s. The students of the original school, which included both children and adults, learned to read the Bible in Dakota first, and later in English. In the early years of the church, religious services were held in the Dakota language, but, by the 1930s, all were in English.

In the 1950s, Oahe Dam was built about five miles south of the mission, which would be inundated when the dam was completed. In 1957, the chapel was donated to the State of South Dakota to be maintained by the State Historical Society. It was temporarily moved to a location on higher ground and was moved again in 1964 to its

Saint Lawrence O'Toole Catholic Church, Central City, Lawrence County, 1878 [7/30/2007]

present site near the east end of Oahe Dam. The Oahe Chapel Preservation Society and the State Historical Society, which now owns the building, restored the chapel in the late 1980s. It is now listed on the National Register of Historic Places.[10]

SAINT LAWRENCE O'TOOLE CATHOLIC CHURCH, Central City, 1878

In 1878, Father B. Mackin, a Catholic priest, arrived in the northern Black Hills and established churches at Lead and Central City in the gold-mining area of central Lawrence County. The church in Central City, two miles west of Deadwood, was named Saint Lawrence O'Toole in honor of a twelfth-century archbishop from Ireland. Soon, however, Saint Lawrence O'Toole became a station church, which meant it had no parish priest and would only be visited periodically by a priest from another church, most often from Deadwood. In 1916, the church was finally assigned a resident pastor, Rev. John Novak.

At some point during its use, an historic bell with silver composition was moved from Galena and installed in the steeple of Saint Lawrence O'Toole. By 1953 the church was no longer in use, but fifty years later, in 2003, it was listed in the National Register of Historic Places. Central City had a population in 2010 of 134.[11]

RENNER LUTHERAN CHURCH, Renner, 1878

Two veterans of the Civil War, John Thompson and Jonas Nelson, were among the first homesteaders in Minnehaha County in 1866. On 26 May 1868, John and his wife, Kristi, had a baby daughter, Berthine Bereline, who was baptized in her parents' home on 11 August 1868. The next day, fifty people joined together to charter the Nidaros Norwegian Lutheran Congregation in that same sod house. The members chose the name after the Norwegian town of Nidaros (now known as Trondheim) in recognition of the place from which most of the charter members had originally emigrated. For the next decade, the congregation held services in people's homes or log schools in the vicinity. On 23 October 1873, the congregation received its first resident minister, Rev. Ole O. Sando.

In 1878, the congregation built its first church on the east side of the Big Sioux River, about three miles southwest of the present-day town of Baltic. The congregation raised thirty-five hundred dollars to pay for the structure. Only three weeks after the church's completion, a windstorm, probably a downdraft from a thunderstorm, knocked the church down. It was immediately rebuilt, but this time with a much shorter steeple, since it was thought that the one-hundred-foot steeple had contributed to the destruction of the

Renner Lutheran Church, Renner, Minnehaha County, 1878 [6/21/2006]

Altar, Renner Lutheran Church

Interior, Renner Lutheran Church

church. The church's wooden altar, built in 1886 by a Norwegian immigrant carpenter named Jacob O. Tveit, is a close replica of an altar in a historic church in Norway.

In 1896, the congregation had six hundred members, although services were held only every other week. There were no bridges over the Big Sioux River in that area, which meant people who lived on the west side of the river often had difficulty attending services. As well, in fewer than twenty years, the original church had become too small for the congregation. Members waged a long-term debate about a remedy for this situation, but no decision was made until after Reverend Sando's death in the fall of 1910. The congregation decided to build two new churches for the parish, one on each side of the river. Both churches were completed in 1911 and were named East and West Nidaros.

Because the town of Baltic had no Lutheran church at the time, the original church was moved there in 1912 and became known as the Baltic Lutheran. The Nidaros parish then included Baltic Lutheran and Renner Lutheran, in addition to the two Nidaros churches, all served by the one minister. Each Sunday, services were held at two of the four churches. All the services were conducted in Norwegian until 1919, when English began to be used sometimes. By the early 1940s, all of the services were in English, except for a few special occasions.

The original Nidaros church was moved from Baltic to Renner in 1939, where it continues to be used as Renner Lutheran Church.[12]

NOTES

1. Herbert S. Schell, *History of South Dakota*, 4th ed., rev. John E. Miller (Pierre: South Dakota Historical Society Press, 2004), pp. 115, 158–59.

2. Ibid., pp. 115–16. Tabor, named after the Bohemian city of the same name, was established in 1872; Lakeport has long since disappeared.

3. Ibid. For more information about the settlement of German immigrants and their establishment of religious communities, *see* Anthony H. Richter, "A Heritage of Faith: Religion and the German Settlers of South Dakota," *South Dakota History* 21 (Spring 1991): 155–72.

4. Schell, *History of South Dakota*, pp. 125–30, 132, 139.

5. For more on the Dakota War of 1862, *see* Gary Clayton Anderson and Alan R. Woolworth, eds., *Through Dakota Eyes: Narrative Accounts of the Minnesota Indian War of 1862* (Saint Paul: Minnesota Historical Society Press, 1988), and Mary Hawker Bakeman and Antona M. Richardson, eds., *Trail of Tears: Minnesota's Dakota Indian Exile Begins* (Roseville, Minn.: Prairie Echoes Press, 2008).

6. Bruce D. Forbes, "Presbyterian Beginnings in South Dakota, 1840–1900," *South Dakota History* 7 (Spring 1977): 119.

7. *An Experiment in Faith: The Journey of the Mdewakanton Dakota Who Settled on the Bend in the River* (n.p., 2003), santeesioux.com; *History of Moody County* (Flandreau, S.Dak.: Moody County Historical Society, 1986), p. 18.

8. Roberts County Centennial Committee, comp., *Roberts County History* (Sisseton, S.Dak.: By the Compilers, 1961), p. 73.

9. Information about the Brown Earth Church is found on the historical marker inside the church.

10. U.S., Department of the Interior, National Park Service, "Oahe Chapel," nps.gov/nr/travel/pierre_fortpierre/oahe_chapel_pierre.html.

11. *Steeples above Stopes: The Churches in the Gold Camps, 1876–1976* (n.p.: Deadwood-Lead '76 Centennial, 1976), pp. 27–28.

12. Historical sign, Renner Lutheran Church, Renner, S.Dak.; *Minnehaha County: Historical and Biographical Sketches* (Sioux Falls, S.Dak.: Minnehaha County Historical Society, 1988), pp. 96–97, 123–24; Dana R. Bailey, *History of Minnehaha County, South Dakota* (Sioux Falls, S.Dak.: Brown & Saenger, 1899), pp. 919–20.

3 : The 1880s

At the end of the 1870s, the population of the area that would become South Dakota was just under one hundred thousand people, but it grew rapidly in the next decade to almost three hundred and fifty thousand by 1890. The end of this decade of rapid growth, the most dramatic in any ten-year period, culminated in statehood for both North Dakota and South Dakota on 2 November 1889. Pierre, in the center of South Dakota, became its capital, while North Dakota chose Bismarck. Because the Missouri River effectively splits South Dakota in two, the land on the west side of the river is referred to as West River, and the east side, East River. Most of the population expansion in the 1880s occurred in the northern and central parts of East River. Brown County led the region in the percentage of growth during the first half of the 1880s. From a count of 353 in 1880, the county population grew to 12,241 in 1885.[1]

The huge expansion of the railroads into East River from Minnesota and Iowa facilitated the influx of homesteaders during the Great Dakota Boom (1878–1885). Settlers began to ride the trains in search of their dream homesteads. The towns built along the newly laid tracks provided water and fuel to the locomotives. Settlers also discovered that the short-grass prairie lands of western Dakota were useful for raising cattle. The open-range cattle industry had gotten its start when Congress extracted the western third of the Great Sioux Reservation from the Sioux and changed the status of the unceded Indian lands in eastern Montana and Wyoming Territories, making them available for settlement. By 1880, there were several hundred thousand head of cattle grazing on public land in what became western South Dakota. By 1884, the number was estimated to be more than seven hundred thousand. Large cattle companies, sometimes financed by European investors, dominated the ranching industry in its heyday, but they began to disappear by the late 1880s, in large part because the railroads invaded the area and settlers began to homestead on the open range, breaking up the vast expanses of pasture.[2] Once the settlers established homes, however humble, they wanted schools and churches nearby for themselves and their families. Eighty-one of the churches built in the 1880s still stand.

CHRIST CHURCH EPISCOPAL, Yankton, 1882

In the summer of 1860, Rev. Melancthon Hoyt, who earlier had founded Saint Thomas Episcopal Church in Sioux City, visited four new towns in southeast Dakota: Jefferson, Elk Point, Vermillion, and Yankton. After his exploratory visits, Yankton was chosen as the site for the first Episcopal church in Dakota Territory. With funds from friends in the East, as well as local donations, Hoyt oversaw the construction of a log building with cottonwood siding at the northwest corner of Linn and Fourth Streets. Named Saint John's, the church was also used as a meeting place for the people of Yankton. When the first territorial legislature met on 17 March 1862, the House of Representatives convened in Saint John's Church. By the time of their December session, a new capitol building was ready for them. Reverend Hoyt, along with his wife and ten children, lived in the church. It was also used as a school and hosted the first Ladies Sociables held by parish women. On 3 February 1863, the congregation began holding its services in the territorial capitol because the membership had outgrown Saint John's Church.

On 23 August 1864, the parish organized and incorporated with the name Christ Church

Christ Church Episcopal, Yankton, Yankton County, 1882 [5/24/2006]

Episcopal. Just two years later, a new church building was built on land at the northwest corner of Third and Walnut Streets, donated by J. B. S. Todd, one of the first businessmen in Yankton. On 25 November 1866, the inaugural service was held in the new church. Built of chalk rock and faced with cottonwood siding, the Christ Church Episcopal was nicknamed "the little brown church" because of its paint color. In 1869, the congregation added a new building, Dakota Hall, near the new church. It served as a school for the community and later as a guildhall and rectory. It was torn down a hundred years later, in 1969.

The second Christ Church Episcopal was built at the corner of Douglas Avenue and Sixth Street in 1881–1882, with the first service held there on 12 November 1882. Two artisans from the church congregation, John T. Coxhead and Alex F. Ollerman, designed and built the altars, baptismal font, lectern, and other interior fixtures. With its stained-glass windows, this traditional church is still in use. Reverend Hoyt, the congregation's founder, saw to the building of fifty-one churches in the area around Yankton. His last church was Saint Andrew's Church in Scotland, South Dakota, where he traveled to conduct the Christmas service in 1887. Soon after, he contracted pneumonia and died on 2 January 1888. For the Episcopalians, this second Christ Church Episcopal was the "Mother Church of Dakota Territory" and a legacy of Reverend Hoyt's service.[3]

CHRISTIAN AND MISSIONARY ALLIANCE CHURCH, De Smet, 1882

On 29 February 1880, Rev. Edwin H. Alden, a Congregational home missionary for southern Dakota Territory, presented the first sermon to twenty-five people on the shores of Silver Lake at the home of Charles P. and Caroline Ingalls.[4] The Ingalls family, made famous by the series of children's books written by Laura Ingalls Wilder, had homesteaded one mile east of De Smet. In her book, *By the Shores of Silver Lake*, Wilder described that first service:

> Pa played the fiddle, and they all sang a hymn. Reverend Stuart . . . made a short prayer for guidance in all their worthy endeavors. Then Reverend Alden preached the sermon. . . . When the team and wagon were ready to start, Reverend Alden said, "You have had the first church service in this new town. In the spring I will be back to organize a church." And he said to Mary and Laura and Carrie, "We will have a Sunday school too! You can all help with a Christmas Tree next Christmas!"[5]

On 20 June of that year, Rev. Edward Brown led the chartering of a congregation in a meeting held in the unfinished railroad depot. The eight charter members, including the Ingallses and their daughter Mary, named their congregation the First Congregational Church of De Smet. A

Christian and Missionary Alliance Church, De Smet, Kingsbury County, 1882 [5/20/2009]

Congregational United Church of Christ, Milbank, Grant County, 1883 [7/16/2007]

year later, on 26 June 1881, the congregation met to discuss the financing of a church building. The national Congregational Church Society offered to donate five hundred dollars to the effort if one thousand dollars were raised locally. Although only two hundred dollars was collected, along with some building materials, the church was built in the summer of 1882. The first meeting was held in the twenty-eight-by-forty-eight-foot structure on 30 August of that year. It was the first church in De Smet, which the Methodists and Baptists also used in the early years. Two years later, the congregation purchased a bell for the church steeple. Made by Henry McShane and Company at a cost of one hundred dollars, it was the first church bell heard in Kingsbury County.

A new church was built in 1966–1967, and the original church building was put up for sale. The Christian and Missionary Alliance, which was first organized as a missionary society in 1887, established a congregation in De Smet in June 1967. One of their first acts was to purchase the original First Congregational Church of De Smet. Significant additions have been made to the church during its lifetime, and it is still in regular use.[6]

CONGREGATIONAL UNITED CHURCH OF CHRIST, Milbank, 1883

Milbank was founded when the Chicago, Milwaukee & Saint Paul Railroad laid track into eastern Dakota Territory from Minnesota in 1880. The town is located in central Grant County, about ten miles west of the Minnesota border. A Congregational minister, Rev. Archibald Hadden of Ortonville, Minnesota, held the first religious services in Milbank on 10 September 1880 in the Drake Store. By the summer of 1881, the Union Congregational Church was organized, and services were then held in the school and in the courthouse. In 1882, the congregation began constructing a church building. Before it was completed, however, Milbank experienced a minor miracle: Jeremiah Milbank of New York City, after whom the town was named, offered fifteen thousand dollars toward the construction of a nondenominational church. For some reason, he later altered his intentions, offering the money to the Congregational United Church, whose building was completed in September 1883. The first service was held 3 February 1884. When the Episcopalians organized a congregation in Milbank in 1887, they too held services in this church building. In 1896, the Episcopalians donated oak pulpit furniture, which is still used today.

A major fire occurred in the church in December 1906, started when a large kerosene-fueled chandelier in the sanctuary fell, causing extensive damage to the interior. After the fire, the interior was remodeled; part of the balcony was removed, and stained-glass windows were added. Until the work was completed in June 1907, the congregation held services in the courthouse and the German Evangelical Church. A basement was added in 1933, although it was not finished until the early 1950s. The church is now listed in the National Register of Historic Places. Milbank boasted a population of 3,353 in 2010.[7]

UNITED CHURCH OF CHRIST (CONGREGATIONAL), Ipswich, 1884

Like so many towns in South Dakota, Ipswich was founded when the railroad track arrived in the early 1880s, and it became the county seat of Edmunds County. The United Church of Christ (Congregational) in Ipswich began as a Sunday school in 1883, which met in the Marshall Store in Freeport, a town one mile east and one-half mile north of Ipswich. The members sat on boxes and sawhorses during their meetings. Soon after this inauspicious beginning, a collection of Protestant churches, including Methodists, Baptists, Presbyterians, Episcopalians, and Congregationalists, came together to form a church group in Ipswich. Because the acting minister at the time was Rev. S. A. Belt, a Congregationalist, the group was incorporated as the Congregational Church of Ipswich on 27 September 1884. Construction began soon after on a thirty-by-forty-two-foot church, which was completed by the end of the year. While the new church was being built, services were held in McNamara's Hall, which they rented for five dollars per Sunday.

United Church of Christ (Congregational), Ipswich, Edmunds County, 1884 [8/16/2007]

Between 1913 and 1918, six stained-glass windows that depict the life of Christ were installed in the church. Parishioners donated at least five of them. A basement and an addition to the west of the building were added in the early 1930s. In 1956, twenty-six new pews were installed. In 1961, the church became part of the new denomination, United Church of Christ, and since then has been known as the Ipswich United Church of Christ (Congregational). In 2010, Ipswich was home to 954 people.[8]

SAINT ANN'S CATHOLIC CHURCH, rural Ramona, 1884

In the mid-1870s, a number of Swiss immigrated to the United States and settled temporarily

Saint Ann's Catholic Church, rural Ramona, Lake County, 1884 [5/28/2010]

in Stillwater, Minnesota, where they formed the Ligia Grischa Colony with the objective of immigrating to Dakota Territory. In 1876, ten members visited the area of northern Lake County in Dakota Territory and filed claims for land around a small lake that was later named Lake Badus in memory of a mountain, Piz Badus, in Switzerland. In the spring of 1878, several of these men, led by Joseph Muggli, began building houses and breaking the prairie on their claims. They also planned to build a church, a school, and a colony house. These settlers spoke the Romansch language, one of the four national languages of Switzerland, now spoken by fewer than one percent of its citizens. The school and the colony house were built in the fall of 1878 from lumber shipped from Stillwater by train to Volga, which was the nearest railroad stop at the time. Drivers hauled the lumber the rest of the way by wagon. The colony house was used for social activities and included a store and the post office. The school, which also served as a place of worship, continued to hold classes through 1948 when a fire destroyed the structure.

Father John Brogan, a missionary priest whose parish was in Madison, South Dakota, organized the congregation of Saint Ann in 1880. Father Thomas Flynn, one of the first Catholic priests ordained in Dakota Territory, became the first parish priest in 1881. At first, the parish was the area between Flandreau on the east and the Missouri River on the west. In 1884, the Badus Swiss and another immigrant group, known as the Nunda Irish, formed a corporation to build Saint Ann's Catholic Church of Badus, completed in the fall. The main part of the church building seated 275 people and cost three thousand dollars to construct. In time, a sacristy room was added to the rear of the church, and a small belfry was added to the front roof. The church is located two miles north and two and one-half miles east of Ramona in northwest Lake County.

Before Saint William's Church in Ramona opened in 1898, splitting the old parish into two

Saint Martin's Lutheran Church, Alexandria, Hanson County, 1885 [7/17/2009]

groups, Saint Ann's Catholic Church had more than one hundred families, mostly of Swiss and Irish heritage. Saint Ann's Church closed in 1965, but the building is still maintained. It has been registered in the National Register of Historic Places and the South Dakota Register of Historic Property.[9]

SAINT MARTIN'S LUTHERAN CHURCH, Alexandria, 1885

In the spring of 1879, Lutherans Ludwig Plagmann and Christ Elfert traveled from Clayton County in northeastern Iowa to Hanson County in Dakota Territory and filed for homesteads. The wagon trip took nine days. Other Lutherans from Clayton County followed soon after. Pastor Melcher held the first Lutheran service in the spring of 1879 in the home of Christ Elfert. Because the railroad tracks had not been extended into the area, all supplies and building materials for the settlers had to be brought by wagon from Sioux Falls, about fifty-five miles distant. When the railroad arrived in the spring of 1880, it did not go through the site originally selected for Alexandria on the James River. Because settlers recognized how important the railroad would be to their community's growth, they moved their townsite a few miles northeast to be on the new line. Alexandria, the Hanson County seat, lies in the east-central part of the county. Its 2010 population was 615.

In 1883, settlers built a school, known as Lehmann's School, in Taylor Township, about seven miles southeast of Alexandria. A parsonage was built in 1891 and was used as a German church school and for confirmation classes. In 1899, Percy M. Rudisill from Spencer was hired to build a church eight and one-half miles southeast of Alexandria. Named the Saint Martin's Lutheran Church, the building served the parish until 1931, when the congregation moved into an older church building in Alexandria.

The Congregationalists had built this structure in Alexandria in 1885. The primary carpenter on the project was Charlie Phillips. In 1899, the Congregationalists sold the building to the Church of Christ, which used it until 1919. The Odd Fellow Lodge bought the building that year and used it until 1931. During their ownership, the lodge removed the steeple and put a basement under the building. As the Great Depression deepened in South Dakota, a bank took over the building temporarily but sold it to Saint Martin's Lutheran Church on 3 March 1931. When the congregation made the decision to move from their country church into town, they installed a stage in the newly purchased building to serve as the chancel and moved the chancel furniture and the pews in from their former church. The building was dedicated on 6 September 1931. They sold the old church, which was eventually torn down and the lumber used to build a house.

In 1951, the bell that had been in the Presbyterian church was donated to Saint Martin's and was installed in 1952. In 1957, the congregation added a forty-by-forty-foot annex and remodeled the original building, all at a cost of twenty-eight thousand dollars.[10]

Redeemer Lutheran Church, Doland, Spink County, 1885 [6/17/2010]

REDEEMER LUTHERAN CHURCH, Doland, 1885

The church building that is today known as Redeemer Lutheran Church in Spink County started its life in Brown County to the north in 1885. Trinity Church, a Missouri Synod Lutheran congregation, was organized in the town of James in Henry Township in southeast Brown County on 30 July 1882. James is thirteen miles east of Aberdeen. In 1885, the congregation built a church, initially named the German Lutheran Church and, the following year, incorporated it as Saint Johannes Evangelical Lutheran Church. Meanwhile, Lutherans in West Hanson Township, south of James, organized a congregation in 1883, and in 1888, that congregation incorporated as Saint John's Evangelical Lutheran Church and built a church. In 1911, they replaced their first building with a new edifice, which burned down in April 1955. Rather than rebuild again, the Saint John's congregation of West Hanson purchased the Saint Johannes Evangelical Lutheran Church building in James, which was no longer in use. They moved it to the site of their last church and remodeled it. By 1968, this Brown County church building was again no longer in use, but its life had not ended.

In 1930, a new Lutheran congregation formed in Doland in east-central Spink County, named Redeemer Evangelical Lutheran. The congregation originally purchased a building formerly known as the Christian Brethren Church. On 25 January 1969, the church burned, and the congregation temporarily held their worship services in the American Legion Hall. At this point, the West Hanson Lutheran congregation in Brown County dissolved and sold their church building to the Redeemer Lutheran congregation for one dollar, including all of its contents. The building was moved to Doland, where the first services were held on 29 June 1969. The church is still active in Doland, which had a 2010 population of 180 people.[11]

SAINT JOHN'S EPISCOPAL CHURCH, rural Oglala, 1888

Little is known about the origins of Saint John's Church, eight miles north of Oglala in what is now Oglala Lakota County. The Episcopalians had formed a mission near Pine Ridge Agency, which they named Holy Cross Mission in 1880, and Saint John's Church, built originally in 1888, was part of that mission complex and is most often referred to as Church of the Holy Cross, although it is also called Church of the Holy Fellowship.[12] Situated near the current town of Pine Ridge, it played a significant role following the Wounded Knee Massacre on 29 December 1890. As a snow storm closed in, the United States Cavalry placed thirty-three wounded Indians, mostly women and children, in wagons and hauled them to the Pine Ridge Agency. For lack of a more suitable place, they were housed in the church.

Before putting the wounded in the church, the staff and volunteers removed the pews and placed

Saint John's Episcopal Church, rural Oglala, Oglala Lakota County, 1888 [9/9/2010]

Interior, Saint John's Episcopal Church

hay on the floor as padding, laying the patients on blankets and quilts atop the hay. The church had been decorated for Christmas, and a sign hung above the pulpit reading "Peace on Earth, Good Will Toward Men." In spite of the efforts of Dr. Charles Eastman and some agency charity workers, most of the injured Lakotas perished.[13] Sometime after 1890, this church building was moved to its current location eight miles north of Oglala and renamed Saint John's Church.

UNITED METHODIST CHURCH, Leola, 1889

Rev. G. W. Hickman arrived in Leola in 1887 to organize a Methodist congregation. On 15 December 1888, the congregation was incorporated, and plans were made to build a church the following year. Rev. Lyle F. Beach was the first pastor. In the spring, the foundation for the church was built. Lumber for the church was stacked near the new foundation. On 2 April 1889, a disastrous fire swept through Leola. Although the town had been in existence for only six years, it had a hundred buildings. The fire destroyed all but a dozen of these. The lumber stacked next to the church foundation also burned, while Reverend Hickman stood nearby and watched helplessly. While the congregation met temporarily in the school, they decided to go forward with their plans. They again purchased the required lumber and then built the church for five thousand dollars. Completed before the end of 1889, church was named the First Methodist Episcopal Church. The town was quickly rebuilt as well.

The first commencement ceremony for the town's school was held in the church in June of 1903, and other education-related functions also took place there. In December 1908, a bell was installed in the church belfry, which beckoned parishioners to worship and also served as a fire alarm for the town. In 1924, an annex was built on

United Methodist Church, Leola, McPherson County, 1889 [8/16/2007]

Congregational United Church of Christ, Canova, Miner County, 1889 [6/22/2006]

the south side of the church. In 1939, the church was renamed the Methodist Church, and in 1968 it became the United Methodist Church.[14] Leola is the county seat of McPherson County and had a population of 457 in the 2010 census. The Leola United Methodist Church is still in regular use.

CONGREGATIONAL UNITED CHURCH OF CHRIST, Canova, 1889

Canova, named for the Italian sculptor Antonio Canova, is in the southeast corner of Miner County. Rev. J. H. Gurney lived on his homestead nine miles southwest of Canova in 1883. On 30 September, he began holding religious services in Canova, first in Osgood Hall, which was on the second floor of a store run by A. P. Osgood, and later in the railroad depot waiting room. Reverend Gurney continued to hold occasional services in Canova until the spring of 1886. In June of that year, Rev. Clarence T. Brown, a student at Yale Seminary who was preaching that summer in Carthage, a town in northeast Miner County, was invited to preach in Canova as well. During this summer, the congregation was organized, and Rev. L. E. Osgood served both Carthage and Canova for the next few years.

In the spring of 1888, under Rev. George J. Battey, a subscription paper for a church building circulated among the congregation, raising pledges of eleven hundred dollars. On 5 July, ground was broken for the church. Members of the congregation hauled forty-five loads of stone and seven loads of sand to the site for the foundation, but construction of the building was delayed until 13 June 1889, when thirty men gathered at the church site and began the building process. On 15 September, the new church was dedicated as the Congregational Church. It had cost $1,798. In the early 1900s, an addition was built on the east side of the church and a basement was added.

In 1909, the windows of the church were replaced with stained-glass windows, many of which were donated by the Sunday school classes. The Sunday school children also raised money for the church bell. Mary Hinman, the superintendent, had arranged that each child be given a nickel to grow over the summer through various fundraising schemes, which they did. On

Thanksgiving Day, the bell was dedicated, and each child was allowed to ring it.[15]

The church is still in regular use in Canova, whose population in 2010 was 105 people.

NOTES

1. Herbert S. Schell, *History of South Dakota*, 4th ed., rev. John E. Miller (Pierre: South Dakota Historical Society Press, 2004), pp. 159, 165.

2. Ibid., pp. 138–39, 243, 252.

3. Yankton County Historical Society, *History of Yankton County, South Dakota* (Dallas, Tex.: Curtis Media Corp., 1987), pp. 121–22. *See also* George W. Kingsbury, *History of Dakota Territory*, vol. 1 (Chicago: S. J. Clarke Co., 1915), pp. 214–15.

4. Caryl Lynn Meyer Poppen, ed., *De Smet Yesterday and Today,* (De Smet, S.Dak.: De Smet Bicentennial Committee, 1976), p. 135. For more on the early history of the church, *see* Laura Ingalls Wilder, *Pioneer Girl: The Annotated Autobiography*, ed. Pamela Smith Hill (Pierre: South Dakota Historical Society Press, 2014), pp. 187–88.

5. Laura Ingalls Wilder, *By the Shores of Silver Lake* (New York: Harper and Bros., 1953), p. 222.

6. Poppen, *De Smet Yesterday and Today*, pp. 135–36, 152–53; "De Smet Alliance Church: The Church That Pa Built," desmetalliancechurch.com.

7. Grant County Historical Society, [comp.], *100 Years in Grant County, South Dakota* ([Milbank,] S.Dak.: By the Compiler, 1979), pp. 34, 95–96.

8. Charlotte Peterson et al., eds., *Ipswich, 1883–1983* (Ipswich, S.Dak.: Ipswich Commercial Club, 1983), pp. 73–75; Earle T. Crissman, Ruth Auchampach, and Beth Crissman, eds., *Ipswich 75th Anniversary Book, "Home of the Yellowstone Trail," 1883–1958* (Ipswich, S.Dak.: Ipswich Commercial Club, [1958]), pp. 51–53.

9. P. E. Tyrrell, ed., *Pioneer Days in Lake County*, Karl E. Mundt Historical and Educational Foundation Series, no. 6. (Madison, S.Dak: Dakota State College, 1980), pp. 43, 89–92; Todd Quinn, Karl Benedict, and Jeff Dicket, "Ligia Grischa: A Successful Swiss Colony on the Dakota Territory Frontier," *Great Plains Quarterly* 32 (Fall 2012): 247, 252, 254; *History of Lake County* (Madison, S.Dak.: Lake County Historical Society, 1995), p. 429; Robert F. Karolevitz, *With Faith, Hope and Tenacity: The First One Hundred Years of the Catholic Diocese of Sioux Falls, 1889–1989* (Mission Hill, S.Dak.: Dakota Homestead Publishers for the Catholic Diocese of Sioux Falls, 1989), pp. 26–27.

10. Mary Ann O'Neill, *One Hundred Years of God's Grace* (Alexandria, S.Dak.: Saint Martin's Lutheran Church, 1988).

11. Brown County Museum and Historical Society, [comp.], *Brown County History* (Aberdeen, S.Dak.: North Plains Press, 1980), p. 122; Leta Anne Nolan, ed., *History of the Spink County Area* (Dallas, Tex.: Curtis Media Corp., 1989), p. 73.

12. This building is called the Church of the Holy Fellowship in Virginia Driving Hawk Sneve, *That They May Have Life: The Episcopal Church in South Dakota, 1859–1976* (New York: Seabury Press, 1977), p. 61.

13. In 1890, Eastman, who had received his medical training at Boston University, was the agency physician at Pine Ridge. Kay Graber, ed., *Sister to the Sioux: The Memoirs of Elaine Goodale Eastman, 1885–91* (Lincoln: University of Nebraska Press, 1978), pp. 161–62.

14. *Leola Centennial Anniversary Book, 1884–1984* (Leola, S.Dak.: Leola Centennial Committee, 1984), pp. 59–60 and "Centennial Book Corrections" (laid in).

15. Canova Centennial Committee, [comp.], *Pioneer Reflections: Canova, South Dakota Centennial, 1883–1983* (Canova, S.Dak., By the Compiler, 1983), pp. 61–63.

4 : The 1890s

The 1890s were quite different from the 1880s in South Dakota. After two violent clashes in late 1890, armed conflicts between the United States Army and the Sioux had largely come to an end. Population growth slowed to a crawl, mostly because East River had been nearly completely settled by then and much of the West River was still reservation land. The population grew from 348,600 to 401,570 in 1900, only a fifteen percent increase. Ninety churches that were built in the decade still stand today.

While the 1880s had been a period of explosive growth, reasonably good weather, and prosperity, the 1890s in general were not as rosy. The relatively dry summer weather of the late 1880s extended into the 1890s. Nationally, deflation drove grain prices down. Furthermore, there were far more farmers in the Midwest producing much more grain than in previous decades, which applied further downward pressure on grain prices. The Panic of 1893 ushered in the worst depression the country had experienced up to that time and led to the failure of many banks, three of the country's largest railroads, and many other businesses, which led to high unemployment and widespread foreclosures on homes and farms.

The resulting unrest among the farmers of the Northern Great Plains fed new political organizations. The most influential was the Farmers' Alliance, which painted big business, high interest rates, and unfairly high railroad shipping rates for farm products as the culprits. The Farmers' Alliance grew into a legitimate political party, the Populist Party, which became an important force in South Dakota politics in this decade.[1]

On 15 December 1890, Sitting Bull was shot and killed at his cabin on the Standing Rock Indian Reservation. Two weeks later, the last, and perhaps the most tragic, encounter between the Sioux and the army occurred on 29 December along Wounded Knee Creek in southeastern Oglala Lakota County (formerly Shannon County), which is entirely within the Pine Ridge Indian Reservation. The mystical Ghost Dance movement, which grew like a prairie fire among the Sioux at the end of the 1880s and the first year of the next decade, had caused a great deal of confusion, fear, and apprehension among the settlers and the army in South Dakota. A part of the Seventh Cavalry had convinced Chief Big Foot and his band of about three hundred forty Sioux, who were already on their way to the Pine Ridge reservation to seek the protection of Chief Red Cloud, to camp near Wounded Knee, a post office near Wounded Knee Creek. While the soldiers were attempting to disarm the Sioux, a scuffle broke out, someone fired a gun, and a fierce battle ensued, even though most of the Indians had been disarmed. Eighty-four warriors, forty-four women, and eighteen children were killed, along with thirty-one soldiers. It is thought that many of the soldiers who died were killed by other soldiers who fired four small cannons into the melee.[2]

As the 1890s went on, the Dawes General Allotment Act of 1887 began to radically change the face of the Great Sioux Reservation. It was intended, at least in part, to remove power on the reservations from the chiefs by reducing the communal ownership of land. Individual Indians were given four years to select their allotments of land, which would grant them eventual ownership of the property. What was not widely understood by the whites of the time was that American Indians had far less interest in land ownership than white settlers in the Northern Great Plains. The land that was not allotted to individual Indians was then declared "surplus" and opened to non-Indian settlement. The Dawes Act was

Hazel United Methodist Church, Hazel, Hamlin County, 1891 [7/20/2007]

modified in 1891 to make it much easier for the Indians to lease their property, resulting in huge amounts of additional reservation land being placed in non-Indian hands.[3]

UNITED METHODIST CHURCH, Hazel, 1891

Hazel is in northwest Hamlin County, in the east-central part of the state, with a population of ninety-one in the last census. In 1883, however, the surrounding community supported two Methodist congregations: one that met at the Dixon School four miles south of Hazel and one that met at the Allen School, five miles east and two miles north of town. In time, they combined and began meeting in Hazel, either in the hall above Bush Store or in a vacant building near the depot.

In 1888, Rev. Henry Springer, a minister who served churches in Kampeska but lived four miles south of Hazel, helped organize the effort to build a church in Hazel. On 28 March 1889, the Ladies' Aid for the First Methodist Episcopal Church of Hazel was organized in the home of Mrs. Charles Kellogg, with Mary Springer elected as the first president. On 5 March 1891, the Ladies' Aid Society began raising funds for a building. Mr. and Mrs. Martin Browley donated a town lot, and construction began during the summer. To help with expenses, the Board of Missions and Church Extension of the national Methodist Episcopal church provided a loan of $250 in October. Late in the year, the church building was completed and dedicated with Rev. J. B. Dibble as pastor.

In part because of the drought in the area in early 1890, the congregation had to wait for furnishings for the new church. They found creative ways to raise money. On the Fourth of July 1892, a chicken pie dinner at twenty-five cents per pie raised $35.32. During that summer, the church was painted and some furnishings were purchased. In September 1893, a Sugar Famine Social raised $13.45 to help pay the minister's salary. In early 1899, the congregation purchased some property next to the church from Martin Browley for $52.50 to be used for a parsonage and barn. The barn was built in the spring and was used as the parsonage while the minister's home was being built. The church had a bell installed in 1905, which later cracked and was replaced in 1958. The church, now called the Hazel United Methodist Church, is still in use.[4]

FIRST PRESBYTERIAN CHURCH, Parker, 1891

Several small towns sprang up in Turner County in the southeast part of Dakota Territory before the railroad arrived. After the tracks were laid and bypassed some of these budding communities, the citizens picked up their buildings and moved them to Parker, the county seat in north-central Turner County. Rev. J. B. Currens arrived in the spring of 1879 and held the first service in Parker that summer in an unfinished store, using boards

First Presbyterian Church, Parker, Turner County, 1891 [6/22/2006]

First Presbyterian Church, Madison, Lake County, 1892 [5/23/2012]

on nail kegs for furniture and a carpenter's bench as a desk. Two women, one child, and about twenty railroad workers attended the service. Subsequent services that year were held in a grain warehouse, the parlor of a new hotel, and the newly constructed schoolhouse. Reverend Currens created a petition to organize a church in Parker and sent it to the Presbytery of Fort Dodge, Iowa, in October 1879. Within ten years, the Presbyterian congregation of Parker grew from the original ten to one hundred members.

The first church building, which became the first Presbyterian church in southern Dakota, was built in 1880. It was twenty by thirty-six feet and had chandeliers, a stove, and carpet. This church cost one thousand dollars to build and furnish, about four hundred dollars of which came from local donors. In 1882, the chimney was moved, and a cupola and bell were added to the building. Several significant donations came from distant places. In 1882, a fine Bible was given by J. B. Broeksmit, an auditor for the Burlington, Cedar Rapids & Northern Railway Company. In the same year, the Presbyterian Church of Big Flats, New York, donated a communion set. A Sunday school class in Troy, New York, donated a Burdette reed organ in 1885.

In 1891, the original church was moved to the country, and a new building was built in its place in town. The congregation dug a basement in 1911, and in 1919, the kitchen and organ-pipe room were added. The organ was installed in 1920. The church is still used in Parker, which had a population of 1,022 in 2010.[5]

FIRST PRESBYTERIAN CHURCH, Madison, 1892

Rev. George F. LeClere of the Board of Home Missions of the Presbyterian church arrived in Dakota Territory in the late 1870s and filed for a homestead a few miles north of Dell Rapids. Initially, he served a church in Dell Rapids and one in Flandreau. He also began holding services in Lake Madison at the Lee Hotel and in a local school. On 31 March 1878, an application was created and forwarded to the Presbytery to establish a new congregation. In 1880, when the railroad established the new town of Madison, originally named Herman, many of the people and the buildings of Lake Madison and Herman moved there, including the members of the Presbyterian congregation. In December 1881, the congregation built and dedicated its first church building. It cost sixteen hundred dollars and had a seating capacity of one hundred sixty. In March 1882, a bell was installed in the church that included gold from a twenty-dollar gold coin that Reverend LeClere had sent to the manufacturer in order to promote a better tone. Because some other local churches did not have bells at that time, the service time of the Presbyterian church was changed to allow the others to enjoy the benefit of ringing the bell for their services. On 8 March 1891, the church burned and the bell melted into a puddle in the ashes. Someone stole the metal from the ashes, and the church placed an ad requesting its return, but it is not known whether it was ever recovered.

The chairs of the church, which were opera chairs, the pulpit, the organ, and the carpet were saved from the fire. Services were held in the city hall and in the Grace Episcopal Church while plans were drafted for a new church. By September 1891, the cornerstone for a brick church was laid. At a cost of six thousand dollars for the church building and two thousand dollars for a new parsonage, the congregation held its first service in the new First Presbyterian Church on 24 January 1892.[6] The church is still in use in Madison, the county seat of Lake County and home to Dakota State University. Its 2010 population was 6,474 people.[6]

HOLY TRINITY CATHOLIC CHURCH, Kimball, 1893

The town of Bendon was located nine miles south and six miles west of Kimball, in Richland Township. It was settled mostly by Bohemians, or Czechs, about half of whom were Catholics. There are no remaining buildings at the Bendon site. Members of the Western Bohemian Catholic Union, who had homesteaded in the area, built the Holy Trinity Church in 1893. Construction began on 1 April, and the first service in the church was held on 17 July. The building is forty-eight by twenty-eight feet and cost fourteen hundred dollars to build. Originally it had a sixty-three-foot-high steeple and was built on a fieldstone foundation. Members of the congregation hauled the stone to the site on stone boats.

The three statues above the tabernacle, those of the Father, the Son, and the Holy Ghost, symbolized the name, Holy Trinity Church. A local artist, Alois Krepela, painted the images above the altar, but, unfortunately, he died in 1913 from lead poisoning, caused by his holding paintbrushes in his mouth when changing colors. The organ was purchased from Dyer Brothers in Saint Paul, Minnesota, in 1904. It cost $3.70 to have it shipped to Bendon. The center aisle of the church was (and still is) covered with a carpet woven from straw. Because it was the only church ever built in Bendon, it was often called the Bendon Church. Most of the residents of the Bendon area, including the author's father and brothers, spoke the Czech language. In fact, many children, even during the 1910s and 1920s, learned English only at school, as Czech remained the language spoken in their homes. Czech priests, including Emil Roubik, M. Pekar, and Joseph Bartick, served the congregation in Czech, but in time, the community could no longer support its own priest. The pastor of Saint Margaret's in Tabor and then non-Czech priests from Sioux Falls served the dwindling congregation.

Use of the church ended in the early 1960s, and it was abandoned for many years. In the early 1980s, Lucille Houda, along with the Brule County Historical Society, took up the cause of moving and restoring the church, with the

Holy Trinity Catholic Church, Kimball, Brule County, 1893 [6/18/2010]

Interior, Holy Trinity Catholic Church [9/1/2016]

goal of making it a museum. After they spent seven years pleading with the Catholic Diocese in Sioux Falls, the church was presented to the Brule County Historical Society, which appointed Houda as director for restoration. By that time, the church had suffered natural damage due to aging. Furthermore, vandals had broken the windows, and birds had taken up residence inside. It was the last building standing in Bendon. The society relocated the church near Interstate 90 on the outskirts of Kimball on 17 December 1982 and completely restored it. The basement has become a museum of artifacts from Bendon and the surrounding area, containing, among other historical items, a row of desks from the Bendon School. The large cross and banner used in funeral processions in the church and cemetery has also been preserved. In November 1983, Holy Trinity Church became the first structure in Brule County placed on the National Register of Historical Places. It is occasionally used for weddings as an interdenominational church.[7]

GRACE EPISCOPAL CHURCH, Madison, 1893

Episcopalians in Madison began holding services in 1885 in a myriad of places: the Boyd School, six miles west of Madison; the courthouse; and the Baptist church. Rev. John Morris from Mitchell and a theological student, Mr. Dairymple, conducted the services. The first confirmation class was held in the courthouse in 1886, and the congregation purchased three lots at the corner of North Blanche Avenue and Northwest Third Street in April of that year. Bishop William H. Hare guided the formal organization of the church in the fall of 1888.

In preparation for building, members of the congregation gathered stones for the foundation from their farms and hauled them by wagon to the construction site. The cornerstone was laid on 6 August 1890. In 1893, the building was completed. It was built from quartzite quarried at Dell Rapids

Grace Episcopal Church, Madison, Lake County, 1893 [8/8/2006]

and trimmed with cut prairie boulders. The pews and pulpit were made of oak. The layout was a Latin Cross (cruciform). It had a seating capacity of one hundred thirty, and the possibility of expansion was included in the plans. The church was equipped with electric lights. In 1928 and 1929, a brick addition was built on the west side of the church to be used as a guild hall. The addition necessitated the reorientation of the interior. The altar was moved from the west end to the east end, and the pews were turned around. This beautiful edifice is still in use.[8]

CHURCH OF THE LIVING WATER (EPISCOPAL), Dell Rapids, 1893

Dell Rapids was founded in 1871 in the northern part of Minnehaha County. It sits near a large vein of quartzite, which was used to construct some of its downtown buildings. In 1879, a few Dell Rapids residents began to consider establishing an Episcopal church. Anna Potter wrote to the dean of the Sioux Falls Episcopal Church to inform him of their plans. The Episcopal dean came to Dell Rapids in March 1880 and conducted a service in the sitting room of the Exchange Hotel. He suggested the people write to the bishop, who visited Dell Rapids and held a service in the Baptist church later that year, establishing a mission named the Gethsemane Mission. On 2 December 1880, the group bought a lot on Pearl Street and purchased a warehouse for one hundred dollars, moved it to the lot, and converted it into a meeting place. A Reverend Morrison became the first resident minister, staying for nine months. After his departure, services were held intermittently by visiting ministers until T. Howell Richards, a lay leader, arrived and became the minister of the mission. A Sunday school and two youth societies, Daughters of the King and Philadelphia Brotherhood, were organized, in addition to the already established Ladies' Guild. Richards was ordained deacon in 1884 and led the mission until 1898.

Construction of a beautiful and distinctive granite church of English architecture began in 1892 on Orleans and High Street. Bishop William H. Hare dedicated it as the Church of the Living Water in June 1893. Perhaps the most distinguishing element of the church is a small stained-glass window in the sanctuary over the altar. Originally a part of the Saint Nicholas Church at Long Station, England, the window dates back to AD 1230, when it was supposedly made for a monastery. Walter Crisp, a member of the Church of the Living Water congregation who had grown up in Long Station, went back to England to visit his hometown and was given the window while there. He brought it back to Dell Rapids and donated it to the church. The Daughters of the King and the Philadelphia Brotherhood societies also donated stained-glass windows to the church. Another youth group, the Chimes Society, was formed for the purpose of raising money for bells. Their effort led to the purchase of the two bells that hang in the steeple.

Church of the Living Water (Episcopal), Dell Rapids, Minnehaha County, 1893 [6/21/2006]

First Congregational Church, Turton, Spink County, 1893 [6/17/2010]

The Church of the Living Water never became a parish church; it was always a mission church. For most of the time that the congregation existed, ministers from Flandreau, Howard, Madison, and Sioux Falls conducted the services. Often, a morning service was held on the first Sunday of each month. On other Sundays, an evening prayer service was held. By the early 1980s, only a few Episcopalians remained in Dell Rapids. As a result, the diocese terminated the use of the church and sold the building to Dennis Hood, who renovated it for his residence. In 1984, the bishop deconsecrated the church. The 2010 population of Dell Rapids was 3,633.[9]

FIRST CONGREGATIONAL CHURCH, Turton, 1893

Turton is a small town in northeast Spink County in the northeast part of the state. Its 2010 population was forty-eight. In 1886, some of the Protestants living in Turton and vicinity began to hold religious gatherings but did not affiliate with any denomination. Initially, they met in a sod shanty about four miles northeast of Turton. When the school building was finished just east of town, they began meeting there. Later, they met in the waiting room of the Chicago & North Western Railroad depot, where the railroad provided the lights and coal for heat. Later yet, they began meeting in a room above Turton's first general store, owned by Frank Kohlman. During the latter period, the group decided to affiliate with the Congregational Conference. In 1892, the pastor who was driving the twenty miles from Frankfort to serve the congregation, began trying to convince the people to build a church. Another factor that promoted the idea was the abundant crop of 1892.

In the spring of 1893, a local carpenter, Ferdinand Labrie, was hired to manage the construction of a church building. Members of the congregation performed most of the labor.

The Congregational Building Society granted the congregation five hundred dollars, and by August, the building was completed and dedicated. It took time, but eventually church members were able to acquire heavy oak pulpit chairs, pews, and a bell, which was cast in England. Students from Redfield College, a Congregational school, served the church, taking the train from Redfield to Turton on Saturday. Because of the train schedules, they had to return on Monday mornings from the town of Doland, eleven miles south of Turton. The extra transportation was a burden to the congregation.

In 1948, the church made an effort to collect the money to pay the five hundred dollars that it still owed to the Congregational Building Society. The debt finally was paid on 29 November of that year. On 2 January 1949, the congregation of the First Congregational Church celebrated with a mortgage-burning ceremony. Two of the early members of the congregation, Mrs. Gilbert Bovee and Carrie Cunningham Taylor, did the actual burning. Mrs. Bovee had first attended the church on the day of its dedication in 1893, fifty-six years before. On 14 September 1979, the church was placed on the National Register of Historic Places. It is still in use.[10]

CHRIST EPISCOPAL CHURCH, Chamberlain, 1894

The first settlers arrived in Chamberlain, along with the railroad, in the spring of 1881. Chamberlain was chosen as the seat of Brule County in an election in November 1881. The town's 2010 population was 2,387. The first Episcopal services were held in Chamberlain in about 1883, and a congregation was organized the next year through efforts led by Rev. C. C. Harris of Mitchell. Initially, there were thirty-seven people, in twelve families, in the congregation. Fifteen of these people were already communicant members of the Episcopal church. The group first met in the Hendershot Building, a store on Main Street. Subsequent services were held in the Baptist church, the Congregational church, and in the opera house. By 1889, the congregation passed several milestones: the first baptism on 12 May for William Ashley Dean Niles; the first confirmation for four members on 12 June held by Bishop William Hare; and the formation of the first Sunday school. Rev. John H. Babcock, rector of Saint Mary's Church in Mitchell, assumed charge of the congregation in 1890, a job he retained for a decade.

Christ Episcopal Church was built in 1894 on the east side of Sanborn Street between King

Christ Episcopal Church, Chamberlain, Brule County, 1894 [6/26/2009]

Christ Church (Episcopal), Lead, Lawrence County, 1896 [7/30/2007]

and Stearns Avenues. It was moved to its present location in 1906 or 1907, at which time a basement and bell tower were added. The first resident pastor was Rev. Elias Wilson, who arrived on 21 October 1906. In 1908, the rectory was built next to the church for twenty-five hundred dollars. In 1910, the congregation purchased a reed organ and installed it in the church.

The congregation, as well as the town, grew rapidly after the railroad arrived. Nevertheless, the church has been without a resident pastor for much of its history. To fill the pulpit, the pastor at Saint Mary's Church in Mitchell sometimes served or lay members served as readers. When the church has a resident pastor, he or she often serves the reservation missions in Fort Thompson and Lower Brule. Although the congregation is small, the church is still in use.[11]

CHRIST CHURCH (EPISCOPAL), Lead, 1896

Lead was settled during the Black Hills Gold Rush of 1876 and incorporated in 1877. It is home to the Homestake Mine, which is now used for deep underground scientific experiments. Lead is located a few miles southwest of Deadwood at an elevation of 5,213 feet. In 1910, Lead had the second largest population of cities in South Dakota. Its 2010 population was 3,124. A seminary student from Connecticut, Rev. E. K. Lessell, held the first Episcopal services in Lead in 1878. In subsequent years, services were held wherever a room could be found, sometimes on the second floor of a pool hall. In 1879, the Ladies' Guild was organized and began work to raise money to build a church. They started by hosting a dinner dance that resulted in $175 for the fund. The first application was made in 1880 to organize a mission in Lead, but because many families left the area in the early 1880s, it did not last long. People again began to move to the area in the mid-1880s, and in 1887, the cornerstone of a church was laid at the corner of Wall and Addie Streets. The building was completed the following spring, and the first service was held on 4 March 1888.

By the middle 1890s, the congregation had outgrown the church, and plans were made to build a larger building. A fine brick edifice was built on Main Street in 1896. At the time, the Christ Church in Lead was the largest church in the Black Hills. To landscape around the church, trains and wagons hauled in dirt from an area between Sturgis and Rapid City. In 1900, a kindergarten was begun in the basement of the church. Before long, Phoebe Apperson Hearst adopted the kindergarten and helped finance its operation. She was the wife of George Hearst, an early owner of the Homestake Mine and the father of William Randolph Hearst.

In 1920, the Homestake Mining Company wanted the land on which the church was built for its expanding operations. The company moved the church and rectory, brick by brick, to the west. The congregation added a steeple and bells to the church. The pipe organ of the church was tuned and repaired in 1956. It has 731 handmade wooden and metal-alloy pipes.

In the early years of the church, the Christ Church Sunday school enjoyed a large attendance, with more than five hundred students at its peak. One incentive for the children was the dollar each received at Christmas from T. J. Grier, superintendent of the Homestake Mining Company. Even in the 1920s, more than one hundred children attended the Sunday school. Christ Church is still in regular use.[12]

United Church of Christ, Wessington Springs, Jerauld County, 1898 [6/17/2010]

UNITED CHURCH OF CHRIST, Wessington Springs, 1898

The town of Wessington Springs was founded in 1880 and platted in 1882. Its most rapid growth began when the railroad tracks arrived from the east in 1903. On 12 June 1886, Rev. Sanford F. Huntley and two theological students, along with some local Congregationalists, organized the First United Church of Christ, which later became simply the United Church of Christ. At that time, the congregation adopted a constitution similar to that of the Congregational church at Plankinton. By the end of June, a council of Congregational churches in the region approved the new congregation in a meeting held at the Methodist Episcopal Church in Wessington Springs. The first service, conducted by Rev. W. H. Thrall, was held on 11 July 1886. Services for the next decade were intermittent.

In January 1898, the church members voted to build a twenty-six-by-forty-foot building. The cornerstone, complete with an embedded box of mementos, was laid on 21 July of that year. The United Church of Christ was completed and dedicated on 18 October 1898. In 1914, the church was remodeled and doubled in size. This change was dedicated on 14 November 1915.

In early 1963, the church council recommended that planning begin for building a new church. This process stretched over more than a decade and resulted instead in a 1975 plan for extensive changes to the old building. The sanctuary and basement were renovated and a new wing was added on the east side. These changes were dedicated on 17 September 1978. During 1980, a new entrance was built, the siding and shingles were replaced, and an external steel bell tower was constructed. The church is still in use.[13]

ACADEMY CONGREGATIONAL CHURCH, Academy, 1898

In 1884 there were two Congregational parishes in the northwest part of Charles Mix County: Colvin Congregational Church in Lake George Township and Church of Christ in LaRoche Township, which met in the Nokes School. At the time, Rev. A. A. Brown served them both. When Reverend Brown departed in 1891, the two congregations called Rev. Lewis E. Camfield, who previously served there as a seminary student. When he arrived, the two parishes consisted of one hundred fifty families spread over an area twelve by eighteen miles.

In the spring of 1892, Fremont Hall, a member of the faculty at Yankton College and a field

Academy Congregational Church, Academy, Charles Mix County, 1898 [7/17/2008]

agent for that institution, visited Reverend Camfield. During the visit, members of the two congregations took up a collection to support education for blacks in the South, which netted twenty dollars. The amount was somewhat of a surprise to Reverend Camfield, and it made him consider that if that much money could be raised so easily for the education of distant students, maybe the time was right to start a local school. Students in the area could not continue their education past the eighth grade, for there were no public high schools. Professor Hall encouraged Reverend Camfield to think about starting an academy, which he did. He traveled around Charles Mix County, which covers 1,150 square miles, interviewing people concerning their interest in having an academy in the county. He was encouraged by all with whom he spoke. W. G. Dickinson of Webster, who was superintendent of Congregational missions at the time, heard of Reverend Camfield's vision and visited him. They called a public meeting where Reverend Camfield shared his dream of creating an academy in northern Charles Mix County. He asked for donations of one thousand dollars and eighty acres of land to start the school. Dickinson strongly supported the request with an enthusiastic presentation. In response, those in attendance pledged fifteen hundred dollars and one hundred acres of land. By 1893, the building was constructed on the donated land, and Ward Academy, named after Dr. Joseph Ward, the founder of Yankton College, was established. The first class had twenty-two students; this increased to fifty the following year. Enrollment peaked in the early 1910s at just under one hundred fifty students.

Church services were held in Ward Hall as soon as it was completed. Before the end of the year, the Church of Christ in LaRoche Township, which had no church building, changed their name to Academy Congregational Church and began meeting in Ward Hall. In 1894, the congregation from Colvin church joined Academy Congregational Church. In 1898, forty-two horses and a group of drivers pulled the Colvin church building to the academy. An addition was built on its west side, and a basement with classrooms was constructed underneath it. Eventually, some cottages and a dormitory for girls were built on the campus.

Ward Academy thrived until after the early 1910s, when public high schools began to spring up. At about the same time, the legislature passed a law to pay the tuition for students in public high schools but not for those in private schools. All that remains of Ward Academy is the large church still used by residents of the area.[14]

SAINT IGNATIUS CATHOLIC CHURCH, White River, 1899

In 1892, members of the Two Kettles band of Sioux Indians living in the White River area, which was still part of the Great Sioux Reservation, asked to be baptized as Catholics.

Saint Ignatius Catholic Church, White River, Mellette County, 1899 [5/29/2010]

Father Florentine Digmann, S. J., visited them and discovered that some of the Indians also wanted a church building. On 8 December 1897, forty acres of land on the Little White River were granted to provide space for a church. A cemetery had already been established on a hill on this property, a little more than a mile west of the eventual site of the town of White River. In July 1899, construction began on the church, using a donation of fifteen hundred dollars from Mother Katherine Drexel, a Sister of the Blessed Sacrament and a wealthy philanthropist in Philadelphia. The Jesuit Brothers of Saint Francis Mission, led by Brother Andrew Hartmann, built the church. They painted the church red, and it quickly became a landmark for the area. Father Digmann was the parish priest until 1905.

In 1921, the church was moved down the hill to the valley near the Little White River. This move was not without its costs. One of the men working on the move, Silas Standing Elk, injured his leg and died about a year later. While the church was in the valley, Grothe Hall was built near it. It was named for the parish priest at the time, Father Henry Grothe. The catechist, Francis Bordeaux, Sr., and his family lived in the hall for many years.

The church and the hall were moved to the town of White River in 1961. A local business in Winner managed the move. Soon after, the parish priest, Father George Stroh, did some remodeling of the building, including refinishing the floor himself. The donations continued. A parish in Fort Pierre brought in pews and a table; Saint Nicholas Church in Valentine, Nebraska, sent Stations of the Cross; the Roberts girls donated a statue of Mary; Tony Borszich of Mission built an altar and lectern. Buildings were also donated. A government-built house was brought to the site of the church from Spring Creek to be used as a rectory. A hall was moved in from Red Leaf, where it had been used as a church from 1955 to 1958 and in Norris before that.

A major remodeling of Grothe Hall and the church was done in the spring of 1981. The new décor was chosen to emphasize the Indian roots of the congregation. Local people did most of the interior design. Christine Fogg designed and painted the decorations on the exterior. She also created the heads on the statues of Saint Joseph and Mary in the interior, which were designed to appear as Indians in form, complexion, and clothing. Fr. Bill Stolzman sculpted the statue of Jesus. Homer Whirlwind Soldier did the woodwork.

Controversy arose in 1966 when a new parish priest, Father Leon Rausch, decided to close the Sacred Heart Church in White River, which had a congregation that was nearly all white. His plan was for the congregation of Sacred Heart to join the congregation of Saint Ignatius. After a good deal of sometimes heated discussion, the bishop decided against the closure of Sacred Heart. Although separate churches for Indians and whites may have appeared scandalous, the decision was made to allow the two groups to have their own approaches to worship and to control the style of their worship spaces. On various occasions, the two parishes worshipped together.[15] While Saint Ignatius Church is no longer in use, the building still stands in White River, near the center of Mellette County. The town's 2010 population was 581.

NOTES

1. *See* R. Alton Lee, *Principle Over Party: The Farmer's Alliance and Populism in South Dakota, 1880–1900* (Pierre: South Dakota Historical Society Press, 2011).

2. Ralph K. Andrist, *The Long Death: The Last Days of the Plains Indians* (New York: Macmillan Co., 1964), p. 348; Herbert S. Schell, *History of South Dakota*, 4th ed., rev. John E. Miller (Pierre: South Dakota Historical Society Press, 2004), pp. 305–6. For a recent study of this event, *see* Jerome A. Greene, *American Carnage: Wounded Knee, 1890* (Norman: University of Oklahoma Press, 2014).

3. Francis Paul Prucha, *The Great Father: The United States Government and the American Indians*, 2 vols. (Lincoln: University of Nebraska Press, 1984), 2:666–73.

4. Hamlin Historical Committee, *Hamlin County, 1878–1979* ([Castlewood, S.Dak.]: By the Author, 1979), p. 76.

5. Turner Auxiliary of Post No. 2821, comp., *Then and Now: Parker 1879–1979, Centennial Book* (Parker, S.Dak.: By the Compiler, 1979), p. 64.

6. *History of Lake County* (Madison, S.Dak.: Lake County Historical Society, 1995), pp. 423–24.

7. *Holy Trinity Church of Bendon* (brochure produced by the Brule County Historical Society, Kimball, S.Dak.); Holy Trinity Church (Church of the Blessed Trinity), south of Kimball, Brule County, National Register of Historic Places Nomination (May 1983), NRIS #83004205, nps.gov.

8. *History of Lake County*, p. 425; P. E. Tyrell, ed., *Pioneer Days in Lake County*, Karl E. Mundt Historical and Educational Foundation Series, no. 6. (Madison, S.Dak: Dakota State College, 1980), pp. 44–45.

9. *Minnehaha County: Historical and Biographical Sketches* (Sioux Falls, S.Dak.: Minnehaha County Historical Society, 1988), pp. 88–89.

10. Dana D. Harlow, *Prairie Echoes: Spink County in the Making* (Redfield, S.Dak.: By the Author, 1961), pp. 113–14; Leta Anne Nolan, ed., *History of the Spink County Area* (Dallas, Tex.: Curtis Media Corp., 1989), p. 8. Redfield College offered both high school and college courses. It opened in 1887 under the sponsorship of the Northern Association of Congregational Churches.

11. *Brule County History* (Pukwana, S.Dak.: Brule County Historical Society, 1977), pp. 66–67.

12. *Steeples above Stopes: The Churches in the Gold Camps, 1876–1976* (n.p.: Deadwood-Lead '76 Centennial, 1976), pp. 35–37; Mildred Fielder, ed., *Lawrence County for the Dakota Territory Centennial* (Lead, S.Dak.: Lawrence County Centennial Committee and Lead Civic Assoc., 1960), p. 161.

13. Jack Marken, ed., *The Making of a Community: A History of Jerauld County to 1980* (Wessington Springs, S.Dak.: Dunham Historical Society, 1982), pp. 177–79.

14. O. W. Coursey, *Who's Who in South Dakota*, vol. 1 (Mitchell, S.Dak.: Educator School Supply Co., 1913), pp. 247–48; *Academy Congregational Church One-Hundredth Anniversary, 1888–1988* (booklet) (Academy, S.Dak: Academy Congregational Church, 1988); Edward C. Ehrensperger, ed., *History of the United Church of Christ in South Dakota* (n.p.: United Church of Christ, 1977), pp. 125–26.

15. *75 Years in Mellette County* (White River, S.Dak.: Mellette County Historical Society, 1986), pp. 556–59.

5 : The 1900s

Changes to the Dawes Act in 1902, 1906, and 1907 all made it easier for Indians to sell or lease their property on the reservations to non-Indians. The 1906 change allowed the secretary of the interior to determine that an Indian was "competent," or capable of managing his or her financial affairs. Competency included the ability of the allotee to purchase the equipment required to farm his or her property successfully. With this designation, many Indians were found competent and were allowed to sell part or all of their property. The Indians were anxious to sell their allotments because few of them actually wanted to become farmers, and few valued property ownership. Also, the Dawes Act specified that any land remaining on reservations that was not allotted to Indians was to be sold to anyone who wanted it, which nearly always meant whites.

The Sioux Agreement of 1889 made about nine million acres of former Sioux lands available for settlement. Further cessions made between 1904 and 1913 added millions more acres to the pool of available land. These areas, in addition to the parcels being sold on the reservations, attracted large numbers of new settlers to western South Dakota. A smaller version of the Great Dakota Boom took place in West River. By the middle of the decade, two railroad lines were built from the Missouri River to Rapid City, one from Chamberlain and one from Pierre. These provided the transportation for the settlers going to the newly available areas. Towns quickly sprouted along the new railroad lines, like they had along the tracks that extended into the northern two-thirds of the eastern South Dakota in the 1880s.

In 1907, the Progressive Party gained control of the governor's office and the legislature, which led to a dizzying array of new laws. Among these was one that required primary elections, rather than candidates being chosen by political parties; another disallowed corporate contributions to political causes; a third required public accounting of campaign funds; and a fourth provided free textbooks to public schools.

Many new structures were built in this time period—new churches West River and replacement churches East River. One hundred thirty-three of the churches built in this decade in the state are still standing. The population grew by forty-five percent, from 401,520 in 1900 to 583,888 in 1910.[1]

SAINT PAULI LUTHERAN CHURCH, rural Wallace, 1901

In the first years of the 1880s, Norwegian immigrants settled the northwest corner of Codington County. Reverend Skjorven was the first Norwegian pastor to visit the area, followed by Rev. Anorlas Nielson. Both of them were Lutherans of the Norwegian Synod. Under the direction of Reverend Nielson, the Saint Pauli congregation was organized on 3 April 1883 under the official name Saint Pauli Norwegian-Lutheran-Evangelical Congregation. During the first few years, services were held in homes, but when a school was built in the vicinity, services were held there.

In 1886, the part of the congregation that lived in Wheatland Township, which is north of the border of Codington County in Day County, and the Saint Pauli congregation both organized Ladies' Aid societies. The initial task of these groups was to raise money for a church. On 14 July 1883, a site was selected for a cemetery and church. Because the area of the Saint Pauli congregation had expanded, a controversy arose concerning the location of the hoped-for church. Meetings were held during 1888 and 1889 to try to resolve the issue while funds were being raised

Saint Pauli Lutheran Church, rural Wallace,
Codington County, 1901 [5/20/2009]

for the building. At some meetings, the members reached an agreement, but they annulled it at the next. Finally, on 5 November 1889, the necessary two-thirds of the congregation voted for the site of the current church, four and one-half miles north of the present town of Wallace in the northwest corner of Codington County. As evidence of the bitterness over the long controversy, eleven families on the east side of the parish and three on the west side withdrew from the congregation when the site was chosen.

In 1890, the Saint Pauli Church was built at a cost of $1,304. But just two years later, lightning struck the church, and it burned to the ground. Around the same time, Reverend Nielson became ill and passed away. The next three years—1893, 1894, and 1895—were dry, and the farmers of the area suffered. As a result, the congregation tabled the rebuilding of the church, and services were once again held in a school.

In 1896, the Saint Pauli and Wheatland Ladies' Aid societies began to raise money for a new structure. In 1898, subscriptions again were taken for a church building. In the fall of 1900, the cornerstone was laid, and the replacement building was completed the following year. Even though only partially furnished, the new church had cost $2,105. Of this, the Saint Pauli Ladies Aid Society had furnished $250, the Wheatland Ladies' Aid Society $222. The Young Peoples' Society contributed $200 and an organ. In the following years, these societies continued to raise money to complete the furnishing of the church.

In 1902, the congregation built a parsonage for $2,567. In 1927, they added a basement constructed under the church for $2,191. For the first twenty-five years of the congregation, all services were conducted in Norwegian, followed by a gradual shift to English. The church is still in regular use.[2]

CHURCH OF THE EPIPHANY (CATHOLIC), Epiphany, 1901

The small town of Epiphany owes much of its history to one man: William Kroeger, a priest turned medical practitioner and patent medicine maker. Kroeger was born in Cincinnati, Ohio, in 1853. At eighteen, he enrolled in the Ohio Medical College in Cincinnati and subsequently earned a doctor of medicine degree. He practiced medicine in Cincinnati for three years and then followed his growing inclination to become a priest by entering the Benedictine order at Saint Meinrad Seminary in Indiana. After ordination in 1880, Father Kroeger became a parish priest in Elkhart, Indiana, where he served for fourteen years. During that time, he also began to involve himself in business pursuits, including a grocery business, a dray line, and the Dr. Kroeger Cough Cure Company. How he ended up in Epiphany in Hanson County, South Dakota, is not clear. Bishop Martin Marty, who had ties to Saint Meinrad, assigned Father Kroeger to the small town of Epiphany, which he had named for the appearance of the Magi at Bethlehem. Epiphany is close to the borders of Miner, Hanson, and McCook counties.

Church of the Epiphany (Catholic), Epiphany, Hanson County, 1901 [5/23/2012]

The first Church of the Epiphany, a small structure, was built in 1883. Upon his arrival, Father Kroeger quickly planned to replace the church with a larger one. The new church, dedicated in 1894, did not last long. In 1896, a tornado completely destroyed it, and Father Kroeger suffered a spinal injury in the event that troubled him for the rest of his life. That did not stop him from convincing the parishioners to rebuild a large traditional church structure. For the time being, they laid a foundation, dug a basement, placed a roof on it, and used it for services.

In the mid-1890s, Epiphany had neither railroad service nor a doctor. Soon after Father Kroeger arrived, people began to visit him for medical diagnoses and treatments. Priests in the Catholic church were not permitted to engage in such practice, but Bishop Marty ignored the situation, at least in part because of the medical needs of the parishioners. Father Kroeger's medical reputation grew quickly, and patients, regardless of religion, began to travel to Epiphany to receive his care. Soon he opened a clinic and took on an assistant, Louisa M. Mentele. She served as his nurse and pharmacist, although her only medical training came from Father Kroeger himself. When Bishop Thomas O'Gorman replaced Bishop Marty in 1895, he informed Father Kroeger that his medical practice was not permitted and he needed to decide whether he wished to be a priest or a doctor. Father Kroeger appealed to the Vatican to allow him to continue his dual role, but his request was denied. He resigned as the parish priest and became known as Doctor Kroeger.

Kroeger's medical practice grew rapidly. He soon built a sanitarium and provided carriages and horse-drawn buses to transport patients from the nearby train stops in Farmer, Canova, Spencer, and Vilas. At the peak of his medical practice, there might be three to four hundred people in Epiphany waiting to be seen at the clinic. Kroeger was also interested in new medical treatments. After the German physicist Wilhelm Conrad Röntgen produced the first X-ray machine in 1895, Doctor Kroeger traveled to Europe to see it and bought one for his clinic. His is believed to be the first X-ray machine to appear in South Dakota.

In 1899, Bishop O'Gorman sent Father James J. Heidegger to Epiphany to be the parish priest. Father Heidegger soon had a large church built on the basement that Father Kroeger had begun. It was dedicated in 1901. In the early 1900s, Doctor Kroeger's health began to fail, and shortly before his death in 1904, he requested and received permission to be reinstated to the priesthood. His estate was bequeathed to his assistant, Louisa Mentele, who tried to continue operating the patent-medicine business and medical practice, but the enterprise soon failed. She sold most of the buildings and equipment from his estate at auction in 1905. The remaining artifacts from Kroeger's twelve years in Epiphany are the church and the large stone cross that marks his grave in the cemetery.[3]

Dell Rapids Lutheran Church, Dell Rapids, Minnehaha County, 1902 [6/21/2006]

DELL RAPIDS LUTHERAN CHURCH, Dell Rapids, 1902

In 1871, the community of Dell City was founded in north-central Minnehaha County along the Big Sioux River. When the post office was established the following year, the name was changed to Dell Rapids. The history of the congregation of Dell Rapids Lutheran Church begins with a meeting to organize the Stordahl Lutheran Church on 17 September 1874. Two years later, at a meeting in a school in Dell Rapids, the congregation was formalized and an application filed with the Hauge Synod requesting admission to that body. At that time, the name was changed to Rosendahl Norwegian Evangelical Congregation, although the church continued to be called Stordahl by local people. For its first decade, the congregation had no church building and had difficulty keeping a full-time pastor.

In January 1886, the Rosendahl congregation met and committed to building a church. Esten Estensen donated two acres of land two miles south of Dell Rapids for a church and a cemetery. Under the supervision of Oluf Lyng, the church was built for fifteen hundred dollars and was dedicated on 14 October 1888. In the fall of 1887, Rev. E. H. Midtboe, who had served as mission pastor in Dell Rapids since 1881, organized a second Lutheran congregation, Saint Peter's Lutheran Congregation. Without a church building, the congregation met in parishioners' homes for years. Later, they held services in the basement of the Episcopal church, the Presbyterian church, and the Danish Baptist church. In early January 1893, the congregation decided to buy a lot for the construction of a new church, but it was not until late December1900 when they agreed to begin the building. Chris, Ole, Ingebrigt, and Gunder Paulson; Halvor Osterkil; Tom and T. P. Sorkilmo; and Halvor Halvorson built this beautiful quartzite edifice from stone obtained from a nearby quarry. The first services were held in the new but unfinished building on 24 August 1902. The church had cost $9,800 to build.

In the early days of this church, the congregation observed the Norwegian custom of gender segregation during services. The men and boys sat on the right side of the church, while the women, girls, and young children sat on the left side. The pulpit was on the right side, in front of the men and boys. This custom may have originated from the early law among Norwegian Lutherans that only the men could vote. It was not until the 1950s that the right to vote was extended to all members of the congregation over the age of eighteen.

Although the negotiations to unite the Rosendahl and the Saint Peter's congregations in the early 1900s had failed, two decades later, discussions led to an agreement. The two congregations officially combined on 29 March 1918, with the Saint Peter's church building designated as the site for worship services.

Rowena United Methodist Church, Rowena, Minnehaha County, 1903 [5/23/2012]

The Rosendahl parsonage became the parish parsonage, while the Rosendahl church building was sold to the Danish Baptists for twenty-five hundred dollars. One part of the agreement was a pledge to enlarge Saint Peter's Church and put a partial basement under it. The addition was fifty feet long, thirty feet wide, and twelve feet high. The basement was fifteen by twenty-five feet. The work was completed in 1923 at a cost of $6,500.

In 1921, an organization of young ladies of the congregation was begun, later named the Lutheran Daughters of the Reformation, whose first major project was to raise funds to purchase a church bell. In the 1930s this group, together with the Ladies' Aid Society, began funding the installation of art windows in the church. By 1944, two large windows and eight small ones had been purchased and installed. In the fall of 1947, the chancel was rebuilt, the choir stall extended, a pipe organ that cost $6,274 was installed, along with new rugs. The church is still in regular use.[4]

ROWENA UNITED METHODIST CHURCH, Rowena, 1903

Most of the lands directly east of Sioux Falls in Minnehaha County were settled during the early 1870s. The first Bible study in that area was held in Madison and Elizabeth Webster's crude dugout home. The windows were just above the ground level, the walls were made of fieldstone without mortar, and the doorway was covered by a small shanty. The only religious study resource the people had initially was a Bible. After a few years, Mrs. Webster bought some additional printed religious materials from a traveling missionary, and her husband built a granary on their homestead. The couple—and the Bible study—all moved into it. A Methodist circuit-riding preacher, Rev. G. D. Hook, appeared in the winter of 1874–1875 and preached the first sermon in the area in the two-room sod house of Mr. and Mrs. Samuel McMacken. Over the next few years, pastors from the Methodist Episcopal Church of Sioux Falls led prayer meetings in homes and held services in the school.

The town of Rowena was founded in 1888, and Methodist minister Rev. C. S. Moore was sent to the new town to form a congregation. He found forty willing parishioners and immediately started raising money to build a church. To this end, the Rowena Ladies' Aid Society was formed in 1889. At that time, services were held in the Rowena Town Hall. For each service, a reed organ was carried in from the nearby home of one of the parishioners. Fifteen-year-old Harry Daniel Webster became the Rowena Sunday school superintendent in 1895, the youngest one in the state. Webster later studied art and achieved fame as a sculptor. In 1910, he sculpted a bronze statue of General William H. H. Beadle that sat in the rotunda of the new South Dakota State Capitol. The state of South Dakota donated that statue to the federal government in 1938, and it now stands in the National Statuary Hall Collection in the United States Capitol.[5]

Second Presbyterian Church, Flandreau, Moody County, 1905 [8/8/2006]

The Rowena congregation held a meeting in 1901 in Mr. and Mrs. Milton Wright's kitchen, where they solidified their plans for a church building. On 9 September 1902, the northeast cornerstone of the building was laid. Both the northeast and the northwest cornerstones contained small mementoes. The first event in the church took place in December 1902, before the building was completed. This sad occasion was the funeral of Miss Jennie Wright who was buried in the gown she had planned to wear at her wedding in only a few days. Because the glass windows had not yet been installed, the openings were covered with cloth to keep out the cold.

The Rowena United Methodist Church was dedicated on 8 February 1903. It cost nineteen hundred dollars to build and was completely paid for by the date of its dedication. George H. Perry, who owned the town sites of Rowena and East Sioux Falls, as well as the granite quarries in the latter, donated the pulpit. During the summer of 1905, two young girls from the congregation, Emma Wright and Burdea Bennett, held ice cream socials to raise sixty dollars for a bell. One family refused to participate because they doubted the possibility of the girls' success. When the bell arrived at the train depot, that same family donated money for the rope to ring the bell, which was presented to the church on Christmas 1905.[6]

The Rowena United Methodist Church closed in 2002. In the 2010 census, the unincorporated community numbered about fifty people. The church has been repurposed.

SECOND PRESBYTERIAN CHURCH, Flandreau, 1905

Rev. George F. LeClere of Dell Rapids led a meeting to organize the Second Presbyterian Congregation in Flandreau on 16 September 1877. During the following months, Reverend LeClere held services, and on 30 June 1878, Rev. A. K. Baird from Iowa formalized the organization. Among the charter members of the congregation were the three Van Nuys brothers and their wives. These men were the brothers-in-law of Rev. John P. Williamson, who had helped start the First Presbyterian Church in Flandreau. The new congregation was established to serve white Presbyterians. Services for the Second Presbyterian Congregation were held in a school until their first church building was completed in 1881 at a cost of about eighteen hundred dollars. F. W. Pettigrew, who had arrived in the area in April 1872 and homesteaded on the site of the future town of Flandreau, donated the lot for the church. He platted the town in 1873.

A striking new church was built during 1905, although it was not dedicated until 18 March 1906. It was built from quartzite quarried near Dell Rapids and modeled after a village church in England. The original church was sold to the Veterans of Foreign Wars (VFW) and was subsequently moved to Flandreau Park. The Second Presbyterian Church was remodeled and rededicated in 1953. It is still in regular use.[7]

Komstad Covenant Church, rural Hub City, Clay County, 1906 [6/8/2006]

KOMSTAD COVENANT CHURCH, rural Hub City, 1906

By 1874, many people from Sweden and other Scandinavian countries had settled in northern Clay County. Some of them left Sweden because at that time only the state churches existed, and the immigrants yearned for the freedom to worship where and how they wished. Initially, settlers in this area lived in dugouts, but they soon built sod houses and eventually wood-frame houses. With few trees in the area, the nearest source of lumber in the mid-1870s was Elk Point, more than twenty miles away, and roads were few and far between. The first recorded meeting of people wanting to organize a church took place on 23 October 1874. This first congregation affiliated with the First Swedish Evangelical Lutheran Church of Sioux City. Beginning in 1875, Rev. J. E. Bodin served both of these parishes. During the first year of services, collections totaled a miniscule $6.42. Four dollars of this was sent to the synod, and the remainder was paid to Reverend Bodin as salary.

In May 1875, five acres of land six miles north of Hub City was donated for a church, and the congregation built on it the next year. For the first two years, the new church was unheated. In 1877, a chimney was built and a stove was installed. In 1878, a barn that could house ten horses was built near the church. In 1884, the congregation decided to create a cemetery. The lots were sixteen-feet square and sold for ten dollars each (or a half-lot at sixteen by eight feet). In 1885, lamps were installed in the church. In 1888, the congregation agreed to pay seventy-five cents per week to rent a local house for the pastor.

In the middle 1880s, discord arose among the members of the congregation. Eleven members left to hold their own services in Riverside Township. They even built a small church one mile south and one mile west of the original church. They called themselves the Children of God's Church. In 1896, the new minister of the original congregation, Rev. Carl Hanson, succeeded in reuniting the two congregations. Subsequently, the newer church was moved to the original building and attached to it. Reverend Hanson wrote the first constitution for the Komstad Church, which made the congregation nondenominational. This status continued until 1954. In 1898, Rev. Nels Wickstrom became the pastor of the church, and his wife became the first female member of the congregation. Prior to that time, only men made up the membership in the congregation, but soon after Mrs. Wickstrom joined, twenty-nine other women followed her as members.

The prospect of building a new church was discussed at a special meeting of the congregation on 31 January 1905. Reverend Wickstrom told the gathering that people of the community had promised him and Gust Norgren, who had assisted him in collecting pledges, $4,757 for a new church. That pledge convinced the

Saint Mary's Catholic Church, Zell, Hand County, 1906 [6/18/2010]

congregation to go forward with the construction plan. One hundred twenty-five people then subscribed and paid $6,292 toward the cost. The total cost of construction was $8,456, including $80 for moving the old building so that the new church could be built on the original site. Gust Norgren purchased it for $300, and the congregation met there during construction of the new church. Parishioners' gifts for the new edifice included a piano, an organ, and a pulpit Bible. The church was dedicated on 27 May 1906. For its first fifty years, the church had no running water, but in 1955 a well was dug and a bathroom was built in the church.

From its inception, all services of the church were conducted in Swedish. By the mid-1920s, they changed all services except one per month to English. By the late 1920s, all services were in English. In 1954, the church affiliated with the Evangelical Covenant Church. This church is still in regular use.[8]

SAINT MARY'S CATHOLIC CHURCH, Zell, 1906

By the early 1880s, a group of Austrian Catholics had settled in an area west of Redfield in what is now southeast Hand County. They named their community Mariazell after the town in Austria from which they had come. They sought to secure a priest who could lead services in their German language. Simultaneously, Bishop Martin Marty was encouraging women in religious orders to go to northern Dakota Territory to teach the Sioux people on the Standing Rock Indian Reservation. In 1883, Bishop Marty asked for Benedictine nuns from the Convent of New Maria Rickenbach in Maryville, Missouri, to fulfill that mission as a temporary assignment. Traveling by riverboat for two weeks, the nuns found the trip to Standing Rock so rigorous and time-consuming that it was decided that it was better and more efficient for them to travel to southern Dakota and establish a permanent convent there.

In April 1883, Mother Gertrude Leupi, Sister Jodoka Villiger, and Sister Radegund Vogel, all of whom had emigrated from Switzerland and lived in Maryville, traveled to Zell (the shortened name of Mariazell) to create a convent and school for the Austrian immigrants. Mother Gertrude had previously established a Benedictine monastery in Switzerland. The bishop allowed them four hundred dollars to build a small structure (sixteen by twenty-four feet) for use as a residence and a chapel. Austrian male residents of the Zell area provided the labor, which they had promised Bishop Marty to do if he was successful in recruiting nuns to Zell. The women moved in on 30 December 1883 and the following year oversaw construction of a church. The first phase was a stone-and-sod basement covered with a gable roof. Funds were not available to build the school they wanted that year, but by the next year, 1885, the school was built, with a classroom on the first floor and a dormitory for students on the second floor.

First United Methodist Church, Mitchell, Davison County, 1907 [7/17/2009]

Interior, First United Methodist Church [9/1/2016]

The convent at Zell grew and prospered for a few years and, by 1886, had reached its capacity and goal of having twenty-four nuns and novices. Then, successive area crop failures caused hard times. The convent residents had great difficulty in heating their accommodations in winter and in finding adequate food supplies all year round. After the initial help from the men of Zell, the nuns performed all the activities of the convent from teaching to farming. In 1887, Bishop Marty offered Mother Gertrude a building in Yankton, where she moved and founded the Sacred Heart Convent, while the convent at Zell continued without her.

The basement church was never allowed to grow into a real church. Instead, in 1905, a large forty-by-one hundred-foot church was built at a different location at a cost of ten thousand dollars. The top of the steeple of the church is seventy-five feet high. The imposing size of Saint Mary's Church now appears rather incongruous in Zell, which has about fifty residents. The large main convent building was condemned in 1963, and by then enrollment had dwindled considerably, mainly because of continually improving public-education facilities. The convent closed, and the Benedictine Sisters left the area. The collection of buildings at the site was listed on the National Register of Historic Places in 1982. As of 2010, the convent still stood, and the church was in regular use.[9]

FIRST METHODIST CHURCH, Mitchell, 1907

Rev. J. W. Lee held the first Methodist service in Mitchell in early September 1880. In June 1881, Rev. A. B. Smart held a meeting of Mitchell Methodists to organize the First Methodist Episcopal Church congregation. The Methodists in Mitchell eventually created the Methodist Hospital and Dakota Wesleyan University.

At first, the new congregation met in a small room at the Young Men's Christian Association (YMCA), then over a saloon, and finally in a school. In 1883, they built a frame church, costing $6,970, which included the lot, the building, an organ, and furniture. This first church was dedicated on 5 August 1883. By 1906, the parish had more than eight hundred fifty members, too many for the original building to accommodate, so they began planning for a new building, with George W. Kramer of Akron, Ohio, as architect. The First Methodist Episcopal Church is a large granite building with an imposing tower in the Richardsonian Romanesque style. At a cost of fifty-five thousand dollars, it was finished in late 1907 and dedicated on 26 January 1908. At the time, it was the largest Protestant church in South Dakota. In 1968, the name was changed to First United Methodist. The church is still in regular use.[10]

Saint Mary of Mercy Catholic Church, Alexandria, Hanson County, 1907 [8/7/2006]

SAINT MARY OF MERCY CATHOLIC CHURCH, Alexandria, 1907

Alexandria, South Dakota, was originally called Clarksville, after Dearborn Clark, who donated the land on which the town was founded in 1880. Sometime later, the town's name was changed to Alexander to honor Alexander Mitchell, the president of the Chicago, Milwaukee & Saint Paul Railway (known as the Milwaukee Road), and eventually to Alexandria. The town was incorporated in 1883. The first Catholic mass was celebrated at the home of Felix Curran in August 1880. When Curran's son, Felix, Jr., became seriously ill, the family sent a carriage to Sioux Falls, fifty-five miles across the prairie, to fetch a priest, Father William Maher, to give the boy the last sacraments. Unfortunately, young Felix died the following month and became the first to be buried in the new Catholic cemetery. A Father Willard held the next mass in a room over the Laidlaw Drug Store in October. In the evening after the morning mass, he gave a temperance lecture at the same location. The first regular parish priest was Father E. M. Hennessy, who was stationed in Mitchell. He said mass once a month in Alexandria until 1883, then more often.

The right-of-way agent for the Milwaukee Railroad, John Lawler, donated one block for a church and its grounds and five acres for a cemetery. The first frame church was built in 1882. With furnishings, it cost fifteen hundred dollars. On 18 September 1905, the church burned, necessitating the building of a new one. A stone church was completed and dedicated in 1907 as Saint Mary of Mercy Church. Members of the congregation built the basement with fieldstone from area farms, while stone for the building itself came from a quarry southeast of town. Tom Wilson cut the stones and Delancey Betts set them. Peter Ries, Sr., managed the carpentry work. Parishioners helped with all phases of the

Saint John Nepomucene Catholic Church, Veblen, Marshall County, 1907 [7/18/2007]

First Baptist Church, Lucas, Gregory County, 1908 [5/21/2012]

construction, as did the parish priest, Father Lauer. While the church was under construction, mass was held in the Independent Order of the Odd Fellows (IOOF) Hall over the Pat Wickhem store. This simple but beautiful church is still in regular use.[11]

SAINT JOHN NEPOMUCENE CATHOLIC CHURCH, Veblen, 1907

Veblen is in the northeast corner of Marshall County in the northeast part of the state. Its 2010 population was 531. The original Catholic church in the Veblen area was built two miles south of the town some time before 1902. Although two nuns lived near the church, the congregation had no parish priest. From 1902 to 1906, priests from Sisseton served the church, attended by both white settlers and local Indians. In 1906, the man who owned the land adjacent to the church discovered that the building stood on his land. He promptly took possession of it and moved it to a position near his other buildings. Having lost the church, the white parishioners immediately began raising funds to build a new one. As one example, John and Rosa Vrchota donated a two-year-old colt for the cause. Although there were only seven families, counting one single man, they built a church in town in 1907 and named it the Saint John Nepomucene Church, after a fourteenth-century Bohemian martyr. Nearly all of the parishioners contributed to the construction work. The first parish priest was Father Kane.

While moving a house near the church, the workers uncovered a good basement underneath it. The church was moved over the basement and enlarged. The new space housed the altar on one end and an entryway on the other. For unknown reasons, the Indians who had been part of the original congregation were not part of the new parish. In 1908, they built their own church, named Saint Matthew's Mission Church, near where the original church had stood. Saint John Nepomucene Church is still in regular use.[12]

FIRST BAPTIST CHURCH, Lucas, 1908

Until 1910, Gregory County was part of the Great Sioux Reservation, although parts of it had been settled by white farmers starting in 1889. On 1 September 1907, Rev. Hans S. Wold and five others met in the home of John W. Smith and organized a Baptist congregation in Lucas.

Services were held in homes until a church was built in 1908. The First Baptist Church was a thirty-six-by-twenty-foot frame building with an imposing steeple over its entry. There were three rectangular windows on each side, as well as one on each side of the entry in the front.

In 1950, the church was moved across the road and extensively rebuilt. The rafters were cut in the center; the building was separated down the middle; and a new foundation was built. The two parts were set down with the addition of ten feet in the middle. The original steeple was removed, and, in its place, they added two battlemented towers to the front of the building, giving it an appearance reminiscent of a castle. The resulting building was fifty by thirty-two feet. In 1973, the battlemented towers were removed, modernizing the exterior appearance. The First Baptist Church is still in regular use, although the town now only has a few residents. Lucas is about a dozen miles northeast of Gregory.[13]

FIRST CONGREGATIONAL UNITED CHURCH OF CHRIST, Redfield, 1908

The first post office in Redfield in Spink County was established in 1880, although the original name of the place was Stennett Junction. When the Chicago & North Western Railway tracks arrived in 1881, the name was changed to Redfield to honor Joseph Barlow Redfield, a railroad company auditor. A minister from New Hampshire, Rev. Albert J. Canney, arrived in Redfield in 1880 and organized the Congregational congregation on December twenty-third of that year, serving as pastor until April 1882.

At first, services were held in homes and in store buildings, but when the trains started rolling, the congregation was allowed to hold services in a passenger coach at the depot. On 15 September 1881, a carpenter was hired to build a church. The railroad donated the lot and the cost of freight for the necessary building materials. By late 1881, the First Congregational Church of Christ was completed and dedicated on 11 December. It was a frame building of thirty by forty feet with a sixteen-foot ceiling and no steeple. Initially, the building was unpainted, and kitchen chairs and benches served as pews. A reed organ was borrowed for the services.

In 1885, the Congregationalists organized Redfield College, which began offering classes in September 1887. Until the first college building appeared in 1888, classes were held in the church, and the president of the college, Rev. David Beaton, also served as the pastor. During his tenure, the church building was enlarged to double its seating capacity. The first college building was an old hotel that was moved from a nearby town. During the early years, the original church also was used by many different local organizations. Suffragist leader Susan B. Anthony once gave a presentation in the church.

In 1908, the congregation built a large new brick church, dedicating it on 25 April 1909. During the fall of 1914, the congregation

First Congregational United Church of Christ, Redfield, Spink County, 1908 [8/14/2007]

First United Methodist Church, Aberdeen, Brown County, 1909 [8/4/2007]

Interior, First United Methodist Church [9/1/2016]

Inside the dome, First United Methodist Church

purchased and installed a Moller pipe organ, dedicated on 27 December 1914. The organ cost $2,750, but $1,250 of that came from a donation from wealthy industrialist and philanthropist Andrew Carnegie. During November 1918, services were suspended because of the Spanish flu epidemic, which caused the deaths of 1,847 people in South Dakota that year. In 1920, a movie projector was installed in the church. Many people came to see the movies, often about missionaries outside the United States, and after each one, a religious service was held (a creative way to increase service attendance). The movies continued until 1928. In 1963, the congregation joined with other Congregational churches to become a United Church of Christ. In 1975, a new addition housed offices and a fellowship hall. The church is still in regular use.[14]

FIRST UNITED METHODIST CHURCH, Aberdeen, 1909

Twenty-five people gathered in Brock's Tent Hotel in Aberdeen on 3 July 1881 for the first Methodist service in the area. At the time, Aberdeen had been platted for a mere six months and contained

Holy Family Catholic Church, Mitchell, Davison County, 1908 [7/17/2009]

only two small frame houses and several tents. The Methodists of Aberdeen held their service three days before the first train arrived on the just-completed tracks. The first minister served congregations in seven other area towns as well. The year 1884 was a seminal one for the congregation, which incorporated, started a Sunday school, and built the first small chapel. Just two years later, they built the first church. Growth in Aberdeen occurred when it became a railroad hub, with tracks coming to town from nine different locations.

In 1908, the congregation began construction of a new church building on Fifth Avenue and Lincoln Street and sold the previous building to the Zion Lutheran Church in 1909, when the new building was dedicated. Designed in Byzantine style, the First United Methodist Church has arched walls and windows and a round central tower. The new church had many facilities, including a parlor with a fireplace, a reading room, offices, a kitchen, a dining room seating two hundred fifty, showers, restrooms, locker rooms, and a gymnasium. In 1976, the church was named to the National Register of Historic Places. The church currently has a large congregation.[15]

HOLY FAMILY CATHOLIC CHURCH, Mitchell, 1908

Bishop Martin Marty held the first Catholic Mass in Mitchell in June 1880. Soon after, Father Patrick Joseph McCarthy organized the parish of Holy Family. The first resident priest was Father Hennessy. A local story holds that this organization took place in a hall over a saloon, where they used planks set on beer kegs as pews. In 1882, a church was built. It was thirty-seven by seventy-four feet, with walls twenty-one feet tall, and an arched ceiling. The church and the lot together were estimated to be worth seventy-five hundred dollars. By 1884, confessions were being heard in English, German, and French, with a mass said in German every Sunday morning at 7:30 a.m. The church was officially incorporated in 1885. In 1886, a school was built, which opened in September of that year with forty-six students. By the following month, the school had eighty pupils. It was founded and operated by the Sisters of Saint Agnes until 1898, when Presentation Sisters arrived. The original school building was replaced in 1912, at which time a high school was begun with the name of Notre Dame Academy.

In 1906, construction of a new stone church in the Late Gothic Revival style was begun. Each quartzite stone used in the building was cut and

Interior, Holy Family Catholic Church [7/10/2008]

Interior, Holy Family Catholic Church

laid by hand. The Holy Family Catholic Church has large Gothic stained-glass windows. The imposing facade of this building includes three steeples, including a magnificent center tower. Bishop O'Gorman dedicated the completed church in July 1908. Father John McHugh Brady was pastor of Holy Family for forty-four years, starting in 1919 and ending with his death at age ninety-four. In 1958, the Mitchell community honored him in a formal celebration for his contributions to the city. One of his achievements was the development of Notre Dame Academy in Mitchell, which at its peak served students from elementary school to junior-college level. Due to economic problems and the shortage of nuns to staff operations, Notre Dame Academy was reduced to kindergarten to six grades in 1970, and the school building itself was torn down in 2005.[16]

In the early 1970s, the Holy Family Catholic Church was repainted and rewired, the pews were replaced, and the original pipe organ was rebuilt. In 1980, several repairs were made to the exterior of the building, including a new roof and stained-glass window repairs. During the first decade of the twenty-first century, the church was enlarged with two additions. Holy Family is still in regular use. In 2009, the congregation included 964 registered families.

CONGREGATIONAL UNITED CHURCH OF CHRIST, Fort Pierre, 1909

Pierre Chouteau, Jr., built a fort and fur trading post for the American Fur Company near the present-day site of Fort Pierre in 1832. The town that was spawned by the fort was the first permanent non-Indian settlement in the state. In the late 1880s, the Sunday School Publishing Society of the Congregational church published a leaflet that found its way to a Nancy Marsh of Providence, Rhode Island. The leaflet stated that a twenty-five-dollar donation could fund a Sunday school in the West; an additional twenty-five dollars would nurture that Sunday school until

Congregational United Church of Christ, Fort Pierre, Stanley County, 1909 [8/18/2005]

Interior, Congregational United Church of Christ

it grew into a church. Miss Marsh was a devout Christian and strongly moved to help. She began saving money and encouraging her acquaintances to contribute to the cause. When she had collected fifty dollars, she sent the money to the state superintendent of the Congregational Sunday School work in South Dakota. He used the money to start a Sunday school in Fort Pierre. Its first meetings were held in an old dance hall with a bar in one end. On 5 March 1890, a small group met in a home and organized the First Congregational Church of Christ in Fort Pierre. Late that year, a building committee was formed to supervise the building of the first church. Sales of subscriptions raised just over two hundred twenty dollars, and the Congregational Building Society granted the congregation five hundred dollars. Several lots on the top of a hill were purchased for seventy-five dollars. In May 1891, the new church, valued at $1,400, was dedicated. The parishioners, however, found that the location of the church on a hill made for treacherous walking uphill through mud to services when it rained or snowed, so in 1895, the church was moved to a lower site.

In 1908, the congregation began planning to build a new church. To this end, an application was made to the Congregational Building Society for a loan of one thousand dollars and a grant of one thousand dollars. Another three thousand dollars was collected in subscriptions from the parishioners, and the Ladies' Aid Society voted to pay five hundred dollars toward the construction. On 12 November 1908, the cornerstone was laid. The church was designed in a High Victorian Gothic architectural style, built mostly from pressed bricks made in Fort Pierre, with a three-foot-high layer of sandstone from Hot Springs along the bottom. The church was dedicated on 20 June 1909. During hard economic times in the 1920s and 1930s, the church decided it would have to do without a pastor because one simply could not be paid. In spite of the difficulties, the congregation and church survived.

In 1962, the pastor, Reverend Gardner, was notified that the church building was no longer safe and needed either to be repaired or demolished. After many meetings, the congregation rejected the option of building a new church. Instead, they began making the necessary repairs, although a lack of sufficient funds left some of them undone. In 1967, when the church again needed repairs, the congregation decided to do only essential maintenance and focus on raising funds to build a new church. By 1972, much of the financing for a new church had been obtained, including a loan of forty-one thousand dollars, but the congregation voted against the proposal to build. In 1976, the church was placed on the National Register of Historic Places. In 1979, the congregation hired a structural engineer to evaluate the church building, resulting in an estimate that repairs and renovation would cost seventy-one thousand dollars. Much of the costs involved improving the structural integrity of the building. Although not all the work was yet completed, services were again held in the church by December 1980. Rededication was held on 22 February 1981. The church is still in regular use in Fort Pierre, which had a population of 2,078 in 2010.[17]

NOTES

1. Herbert S. Schell, *History of South Dakota*, 4th ed., rev. John E. Miller (Pierre: South Dakota Historical Society Press, 2004), pp. 252–62, 311–12.

2. History of the Saint Pauli Congregation, 3 Apr. 1883–1933, from a plaque in the church steeple.

3. Robert F. Karolevitz, *With Faith, Hope and Tenacity: The First One Hundred Years of the Catholic Diocese of Sioux Falls, 1889–1989* (Mission Hill, S.Dak.: Dakota Homestead Publishers for the Catholic Diocese of Sioux Falls, 1989), pp. 89–93; Doane Robinson, *History of South Dakota*, 2 vols. (Indianapolis: B. F. Bowen & Co., 1904), 2:1856–57. A historical marker in Epiphany also outlines Father Kroeger's importance to the town. For more on his life, *see* James Marten, "A Medical Entrepreneur Goes West: Father William Kroeger in South Dakota, 1893–1904," *South Dakota History* 21 (Winter 1991): 333–61.

4. "Pioneer History," Lutheran Church of Dell Rapids, lcdr-sd.org, pp. 7–9; *Minnehaha County: Historical and Biographical Sketches* (Sioux Falls, S.Dak.: Minnehaha County Historical Society, 1988), pp. 9–10, 92–93.

5. Beadle was a civil engineer who rose to the rank of brigadier general during the Civil War. In 1869, he was appointed surveyor-general of Dakota Territory.

6. *Minnehaha County*, pp. 112–13.

7. *History of Moody County* (Flandreau, S.Dak.: Moody County Historical Society, 1986), p. 20.

8. "A Historical Sketch," Komestad Covenant Church, komstadchurch.org; Herbert S. Schell, *History of Clay County, South Dakota* (Vermillion, S.Dak.: Clay County Historical Society, 1976), pp. 149–50.

9. Scott Heidepriem, *Bring on the Pioneers!: History of Hand County* (Miller, S.Dak.: By the Author, 1978), p. 103; Karolevitz, *With Faith, Hope and Tenacity*, p. 61.

10. *Mitchell Re-discovered: A Centennial History, 1981* (Mitchell, S.Dak.: Mitchell Centennial History Committee, 1980), p. 57; David Erpestad and David Wood, *Building South Dakota: A Historical Survey of the State's Architecture to 1945*, Historical Preservation Series, no. 1 (Pierre: South Dakota Historical Society Press, 1997), p. 64.

11. Mildred Soladay, *Hanson Heritage: A History of Hanson County, South Dakota* (Fulton, S.Dak.: By the Author, 1975), p. 102.

12. *Marshall County, South Dakota* (Britton, S.Dak.: Marshall County Historical Society, 1979), p. 379; Karolevitz, *With Faith, Hope and Tenacity*, p. 199.

13. Adeline S. Gnirk, *The Saga of Sully Flats* (Burke, S.Dak.: By the Author, 1977), pp. 71–72.

14. Leta Anne Nolan, ed., *History of the Spink County Area* (Dallas, Tex.: Curtis Media Corp., 1989), p. 67; Dana D. Harlow, *Prairie Echoes: Spink County in the Making* (Redfield, S.Dak.: By the Author, 1961), p. 237,

15. Brown County Museum and Historical Society, [comp.], *Brown County History* (Aberdeen, S.Dak.: North

Plains Press, 1980), p. 237; Troy McQuillen, *Images of America: Aberdeen* (Charleston, S.C.: Arcadia Publishing, 2013), p. 117.

16. *Mitchell Re-discovered*, pp. 56–57; Karolevitz, *With Faith, Hope and Tenacity*, pp. 38, 122; "The History of Catholic Education in Mitchell," Mitchell Foundation for Catholic Education, sites.google.com/site/Mitchell/history.

17. Elda Corey and Jessie Whitney, *History of the Congregational United Church of Christ* (pamphlet) (Fort Pierre: Congregational United Church of Christ, 1990).

6 : The 1910s

Lands on the South Dakota reservations continued to be transferred from Indian ownership to white ownership during the 1910s. The Pine Ridge Act of 1910 opened Bennett County, which had been the east end of the Pine Ridge reservation, to settlement under the general provisions of the homestead laws. Any land that was classified as timberland and land that had been allotted to Indians was exempt from settlement. Bennett County has 1,191 square miles of mostly prairie land. In 1911, the area north of Bennett County, known as Washabaugh County (now Jackson County), was opened for settlement. As in Bennett County, any land that was already an Indian allotment was exempt. The policies of Franklin K. Lane, the United States secretary of the interior from 1913 until 1920, made it much easier for Indian allotments to be converted to Indian ownership. The result was that many American Indians obtained complete ownership to their land, and they sold or leased much of that land to white farmers, having no tradition of individual land ownership.

Peter Norbeck, a member of the Progressive Party, was elected governor of South Dakota in 1916. Early the following year, the governor proposed an expansive slate of new initiatives. A number of them dealt with moving the state into various business ventures, including a rural-credit organization, which would provide loans to farmers, state crop insurance, a state coal mine, and state grain elevators. Finally, he asked for a workmen's compensation law and a project to expand the state's road system; the legislature accepted many of these proposals. They quickly set up a rural-credit operation, enacted a workmen's compensation bureau, and created a state highway department.

Late in the decade, the United States entered World War I (April 1917), and in May 1918, a special session of the state legislature enacted a collection of laws related to wartime. Among these were laws that required instruction in patriotism and prohibited instruction in any foreign language in public schools. Furthermore, the South Dakota Council of Defense demanded that the German language not be used in public conversation or over the phone, except in emergency situations. Many churches used German in their services, and those congregations vigorously protested these measures. In response, the council decided to allow a fifteen-minute summary of sermons to be presented in German at the end of each church service. Local defense councils also used heavy-handed methods to force people to purchase war bonds. Because of their refusal to participate in such activities, the seventeen Hutterite colonies in the state were especially targeted. In two counties, cattle belonging to the Hutterite communities were stolen and sold, with the proceeds returned to the owners after contributions to the war effort were deducted. There was also an effort to cancel the articles of incorporation under which the Hutterites ran their colonies. As a result of such harassment, all but one of the colonies sold their property and moved to Canada.[1]

The decade produced 168 churches that still stand, the highest number from any decade before 1930. The population grew by only nine percent, from 585,888 in 1910 to 636,547 in 1920.

SAINT JOHN'S LUTHERAN CHURCH, Agar, 1910

Agar, originally named Waterford, is a small unincorporated community in north-central Sully County in the central part of South Dakota. In the 1880s, Rev. Ottomar Kloeter walked seventy-five miles from Wolsey, in west-central Beadle County, to hold the first religious services in northern Sully

Saint John's Lutheran Church, Agar, Sully County, 1910
[5/20/2008]

County. In 1890, Rev. Justus Naumann, pastor of a congregation north of Harrold in northwest Hughes County, served the Lutherans in the Agar area. The first resident pastor was Rev. H. Ohldag, who organized the Lutheran group there as Saint John's Congregation in 1894. Largely of German ancestry, the members worshiped in the German language, holding services in area homes for the first fourteen years. In May 1909, the congregation decided to build a church. On 20 July 1909, Mr. and Mrs. A. J. Rogers of Washington County, Iowa, donated a lot one-half mile east of Agar, and by early the next year, church construction was completed. A wagon pulled by a single team over primitive roads brought an eighteen-thousand-pound bell from Gettysburg, about fifteen miles northeast of Agar.

The World War I years proved difficult for the congregation, whose members were forced to begin using English in their services. Although the parish had little expendable cash, they were required to purchase new hymn books in English. The repeated crop failures and dust storms of the 1930s forced at least ten families of the congregation to move away, further eroding the economic condition of the parish. Church records show that budgets for 1940 through 1944 were $446, $439, $728, $822, and $1,302.

On 22 January 1947, the church was moved to town and placed on a foundation that included a basement, which had long been needed to support social and recreational activities. At the time of the move, the steeple was modified, substantially reducing its height. Although Saint John's Lutheran Church in Agar was still in use when the accompanying photograph was taken in 2008, it has since closed. The population of the town in 2010 was seventy-six.[2]

CANTON LUTHERAN CHURCH, Canton, 1910

Canton, on the Big Sioux River about twenty miles south of Sioux Falls, was founded in the middle 1860s. Its founders named it Canton because they believed it was situated diametrically opposite the city of the same name in China. It is the seat of Lincoln County. In 2010, the population was 3,057, but in 1868, the entire population of Lincoln County was fewer than one hundred until June of that year, when a train of covered wagons arrived in Canton with twenty-three Norwegian families who intended to homestead in the area. In October, Rev. Emil Christensen met with fourteen Norwegian immigrants in a log house and founded Canton Norwegian Evangelical Lutheran Congregation, the first religious organization in Lincoln County. For the first few years, services were held in homes, the log community building, a school, and the courthouse. The pastor, Rev. Ellef Olson, also served other area congregations, holding services in Canton once or twice a month. Because funds were scarce, the congregation filed homestead papers for the pastor in lieu of a regular salary.

In 1870, some evangelists from the Augustana Lutheran Synod visited Canton, and a second

Canton Lutheran Church, Canton, Lincoln County, 1910 [6/19/2006]

Lutheran congregation formed in town. On 1 June 1872, the Bethlehem Lutheran Congregation was founded in the home of J. M. Wahl. In 1874, this new group began building a church, but it was never completed. The region suffered three years of grasshopper infestations, which crippled the local farm economy. On top of that, a windstorm knocked down the partially built building. By the early 1880s, the economic health of the congregation had recovered, and they built a frame church in 1882. Earlier in 1882, the Canton Norwegian Evangelical Lutheran Congregation had built the first frame church in town, a traditional building with Gothic windows and a tall steeple. In 1884, the Bethlehem Congregation convinced the Augustana Synod to move what came to be called Augustana College from Beloit, Iowa, to Canton.

In 1890, the parent synods of the two Lutheran churches in Canton joined to form the United Norwegian Lutheran Church in America. One might assume that this union would also mean a merger of the two Canton congregations, but it took twelve years to accomplish that. The Evangelical Lutheran had about two hundred fifty members, compared to the six hundred members of Bethlehem Lutheran, and feared that the larger congregation would dominate. Although both congregations had recently built churches, neither was large enough for both. A larger church structure was obviously needed, but the two groups could not agree on a location. In addition, there were differences in the liturgies of the two synods and the question of which synod would provide the pastor for the merged congregation. In 1902, the president of Augustana College, Anthony Tuve, negotiated an agreement between the two congregations, and the merger finally happened. Until construction of a new building could begin, the Evangelical church was moved to the location of the Bethlehem church, and the two were joined, side by side. The adjacent walls were removed to create a single large nave. The new congregation had 410 voting members, who were all men over the age of twenty-one. It was not until 1912 that women of the congregation were granted the right to vote.

In 1905, an architect was hired to begin designing the new church, which was to be built from quartzite, seat at least eight hundred, and have no center aisle. After the two congregations conjoined their buildings, each of them sat on their respective sides of the church with virtually no mixing. Without a central aisle, the new building would avoid encouraging that kind of

Interior, Canton Lutheran Church

denominational segregation. The women of the congregation were also pleased with the plan. Early Norwegian churches had separated men and women on opposite sides of the church, and the women were ready to have their families sit together.

Construction began in the fall of 1907 with the excavation for the basement and foundation. The quartzite came from the Dell Rapids quarry by train. Members of the congregation hauled the stone from the depot to the building site in wagons. Before winter arrived, the foundation was complete and the walls had risen to the bottom of the window openings on the main floor. During the winter, more stone was cut and marked in preparation for the stone-setting process. On 17 May 1908, a ceremony was held to lay the cornerstone of the church. A crowd estimated at one thousand attended, although no stone was set because shipment of the cornerstone had been delayed. The next day members of the congregation began dismantling the two wooden churches; the wood would be used in construction of the new church. Services were held in the Old Main building of Augustana College until the new building was completed. By December 1908, the exterior structure of the building was completed, and the basement was sufficiently finished so that the Sunday school Christmas program could be held there. The finishing work on the interior was done in 1909, and by late fall, services were held in the church. The dedication of the church was planned before the end of the year, but when the pews and the pipe organ did not arrive, the dedication was postponed until 29 May 1910.

Members of the congregation had performed much of the work on the construction. Farmers worked during the days when they could, and members in town worked in the evenings. They also hired a few common laborers at two and a half dollars to three dollars per day, as well as some skilled workers. Stone masons earned fifty-five cents per hour. Except for a horse-powered winch that was used to hoist stone and heavy beams into the building, nearly all construction was done by hand. The new wood used in the building came from the forest in Newton Hills, six miles south of Canton along the Big Sioux River. At the time of the dedication, the church was the largest in the synod. The donated labor reduced total cost, which was $34,377, of which only eight thousand dollars was borrowed. On the day of dedication, the congregation collected five thousand dollars. Within three years, the church was debt free.

Although some evening services in the early part of the twentieth century were conducted in English, all others were in Norwegian. In 1918, in part due to language restrictions created because of World War I, the parishioners voted to have every other Sunday morning service in English, but the evening service was still in Norwegian. English-only services were finally implemented in the late 1920s, which encouraged more non-

Endeavor Presbyterian Church, Fedora, Miner County, 1911 [8/7/2006]

Interior, Endeavor Presbyterian Church

Norwegians to join the congregation. The church is still in regular use.[3]

ENDEAVOR PRESBYTERIAN CHURCH, Fedora, 1911

Fedora is an unincorporated community in west-central Miner County that began attracting citizens in the 1880s. Some of the first were Evan and Katie (Williams) Morgans and their infant son who arrived and settled north of Fedora in early 1882. A few months later, the first Sunday school and prayer meeting of the group that became the Endeavor congregation was held in the couple's home. In June 1883, Presbyterian minister Rev. Richard Isaac from Lime Springs, Iowa, incorporated the new congregation. For some years, they met in the Lewis school a few miles northeast of Fedora.

In December 1889, Rev. H. P. Carson organized the Endeavor Presbyterian Church, and on 6 May 1904, the congregation of the Endeavor Sunday school agreed to move to Fedora and join with the Sunday school there. Incorporated on 10 April 1909, the joined congregations voted to build a church after meeting previously in schools, homes, and the town hall. Three lots were purchased for the church in 1909. Peter Helland was the lead carpenter for the construction with community men providing much of the labor. Horse-drawn stone boats hauled field stone to the site for the foundation. The church construction was completed in February 1911 and the Endeavor Presbyterian Church of Fedora was dedicated on 5 March. The church is still in regular use.[4]

UNITED METHODIST CHURCH, Egan, 1911

Egan is a small town on the Big Sioux River in central Moody County in the east-central part of the state. Founded in 1880, it was named after a Milwaukee Road official, John M. Egan. Rev. J. W. Dibble was sent to Egan in 1880 to help the settlers organize a Methodist congregation and build a church. The First Methodist Episcopal Church of Egan was incorporated and chartered on 7 June 1881, and a church was built soon after. Because of continuing growth of the congregation, in 1911 the congregation built a new church one block north of the original building. The name of the church was changed to Methodist in 1939 and United Methodist in 1971. After 1911, the first church building became the first and second

United Methodist Church, Egan, Moody County, 1911 [8/9/2006]

United Methodist Church, Wessington Springs, Jerauld County, 1913 [7/8/2008]

grades of the Egan public school until 1922. The congregation of Redeemer Lutheran then bought the building and used it until 1961. After that, the American Legion occupied the building.

In 1881, John Egan had offered to donate a bell to the first church built in Egan that bore his name. The Baptist church was completed first, so it got the 630-pound bell. When the Baptist church disbanded in 1912, the bell was placed in storage and subsequently stolen. Eventually, the bell was recovered and given to the United Methodist Church. John Gueffroy of Colman designed and built an external metal tower for the bell, dedicated in 1977. The church is still in regular use. The 2010 population of Egan was 278.[5]

UNITED METHODIST CHURCH, Wessington Springs, 1913

Rev. A. B. Smart came to the central part of Jerauld County from Illinois in 1880. Impressed with the beauty and variety of scenery around the springs in what became Wessington Springs, he returned to Illinois and then came back to Jerauld County, bringing with him some people who shared his religious beliefs. Reverend Smart built a dugout for himself and began preaching to people who gathered there. On 14 November 1880, he began the process of organizing the first church congregation in the area, but it was not until 8 April 1882 that he formally organized the Methodist Episcopal Church of Wessington Springs. For the first two years, the congregation held services in homes.

In 1884, they built a small church at a cost of fifteen hundred dollars and dedicated it on 27 September of that year. A precursor of the Ladies Aid, called the Ladies Mite Society, donated the carpeting and the organ. As the town of Wessington Springs grew so did the congregation, and by 1902, they had outgrown the church building, replacing it with a larger frame building. The first decade of the twentieth century saw even more rapid growth in central Jerauld County. In response, the United Methodist Congregation undertook the construction of a larger brick church building designed by architect J. K. Snyder. This building, which cost forty thousand dollars, was completed in 1913. It included stained-glass windows; the small ones are Romanesque, and the large ones are Gothic.

Music was always a large part of the activities of the church. Between 1914 and 1921, an

Immanuel Lutheran Church, rural Dimock, Douglas County, 1914 [6/23/2006]

orchestra performed for Sunday school and at the evening services. Musical presentations for the whole Wessington Springs community were frequently held at the church. The first Sunday school in Wessington Springs was organized by the United Methodist Congregation in 1886, starting with about twenty-five members. In the early 1920s, that number had grown to more than five hundred. In 1919, a two-story pastor's residence was built just north of the church at a cost of thirteen thousand dollars. In 1968, the congregation hired the Gilmore Glass Company to reinforce, clean, and repair the stained-glass windows for a cost of almost eight thousand dollars. The church is still in regular use.[6]

IMMANUEL LUTHERAN CHURCH, rural Dimock, 1914

Of the settlers that began arriving in Hutchinson and Douglas counties in the early 1880s, many were German Lutherans. Those who settled in the area about twenty-five miles southwest of Mitchell decided to establish a congregation of the Missouri Synod of Lutherans. Initially, they had difficulty attacting a resident minister. By the fall of 1882, however, they succeeded in hiring Pastor J. Bernthal who, with twenty-three families, organized the Evangelical Lutheran Immanuel Congregation, Unaltered Augsburg Confession. In the spring of 1883, they built a parsonage where they held services, located eight miles west of Dimock. When Candidate M. Waechter became the minister in 1887, they began holding services in a school across the road from the parsonage. Soon they outgrew the school and decided to build their first church. The cornerstone was laid in the spring of 1889, and the church was dedicated on September twenty-second of the same year. The building had cost one thousand dollars. The congregation added a bell in 1892 and an organ in 1895.

In 1903, a church school was built near the parsonage. In 1917, the school building was moved to five acres that had been donated near the church. At the same time, the congregation enlarged the structure by relocating a house next to the school and joining them together. The new building was used as lodging for teachers and to hold some classes. The other classes were held in the church basement. The classes in Catechism, Bible history, reading, and writing were taught in German, while other subjects were taught in English. The school did not last long. When the school's second teacher left in 1921, it was closed, and religious instruction was relegated to the Sunday school. In 1927, the school building was sold.

By 1913, the congregation had outgrown the original church. The pastor, Rev. P. Hempel, conducted a door-to-door donation drive and soon had pledges of more than ten thousand dollars, the estimated cost of the new building. The old

First United Methodist Church, Watertown, Codington County, 1915 [7/20/2007]

Interior, First United Methodist Church [9/1/2016]

church was moved to the side, and the cornerstone of a large new church, ninety by forty feet, was laid on 26 April 1914. The steeple of the church is 110 feet high. It was dedicated on 30 August 1914 and had 318 members.

World War I brought anti-German sentiment to the state and nation. Because he preached in the German language, Pastor Hempel was arrested on 15 January 1918 and held in Fort Douglas, Utah, for eighteen months. The congregation took care of his family during his absence. Although he had been ordered not to continue preaching in German when he was released in June 1919, he defiantly refused to conduct services in English. The Spanish influenza epidemic also took its toll on members of the congregation.

In 1926, the congregation purchased a pipe organ for three thousand dollars. In the late 1920s and the 1930s, several windstorms caused the church to lean to the east. Placing steel posts on either side of the building and running steel cable across the nave corrected the problem. Over its whole lifetime, the Immanuel Lutheran Church has been well maintained and has undergone numerous improvements and modernizations. The church is still in regular use.[7]

FIRST UNITED METHODIST CHURCH, Watertown, 1915

Watertown was incorporated on 30 May 1880 and named after Watertown, New York, the hometown of two town founders, brothers John E. and Oscar P. Kemp. One of the first circuit rider preachers to venture into Codington County was a Congregationalist, Rev. George S. Codington, for whom the county was named. The first church established in Watertown was a Congregational church, organized in March 1879.

Rev. Albon D. Chase held the first Methodist service near Watertown in the home of D. M. Richardson in May 1878. By late 1879, Reverend Chase had organized the Watertown Methodist Episcopal Church. In the same year, a Methodist parsonage was built, and services were held in a school. Starting in 1880, services were held every two weeks in Gesley's Hall. A small church was built the same year, with the financial help of the Church Extension Society of the national Congregational church. By 1888, the congregation had 204 members, and the building had become too small. A lot was purchased where the parsonage was relocated, and a new church was built on the lot for fifteen thousand dollars. The congregation had raised ten thousand dollars for the construction.

Union Presbyterian Church, rural Canova, Miner County, 1915 [5/23/2012]

Some of the homesteaders in the Watertown area left during the early 1890s because of the poor economy, successive droughts, and grasshopper infestations. In 1893, however, eight railroads and eight newspapers served about six thousand people in Watertown. In the early 1900s, the congregation built a new parsonage for about thirty-five hundred dollars, and the old one was sold.

The congregation continued to grow during the first decade of the twentieth century. By 1911, talks began about the need for a new larger church; by early 1914, the congregation had raised forty-seven thousand dollars in pledges. In June 1914, Brickell Construction was hired to build the church, and architect Harry Jones of Minneapolis managed the construction. The old church was razed, and a new church rose up in its place. During construction, the Watertown Methodist Episcopal congregation met in the theater of the Lincoln Hotel. Built of sandstone, the church was a Gothic style and cost seventy-five thousand dollars. It was dedicated on 17 October 1915. The building included a large auditorium, shared with the community for various activities. The church's gymnasium was used by local schools until the high school was built in 1923. The impressive First United Methodist Church has been well maintained and is still in regular use.[8]

UNION PRESBYTERIAN CHURCH, rural Canova, 1915

Rev. R. W. Jones began holding Sunday school meetings in homes in the southeast part of Miner County in the spring of 1883. In June, Rev. W. S. Peterson joined this group in the home of Thomas Williams and organized a congregation with the name Union Presbyterian. The first church building was built in 1884. That church, as well as the next, was located three miles north and five miles east of Canova in Vermillion Township.

In 1915, they tore down the old church and built a larger one, complete with a basement containing a kitchen and a dining room. The new church was dedicated on 15 August, completely debt free. Perhaps the most architecturally interesting part of the church is the five-sided front of the right wing of the structure. In the early days of this church, music was important to the congregation. A male quartet and a large mixed chorus, called the Choral Union, helped provide music for the worship services. The occasionally severe weather of the Northern Great Plains affected the services schedule of this rural church. For example, because snow blocked all roads leading to the church between 27 January and 24 March 1929, no services were held for two months. On 12 November 1933, services were cancelled because of a severe dust storm.

The Great Depression affected everyone in the country, including Union Presbyterian Church congregation. In 1935, when money was scarce, members donated some of their grain crops, which were then sold and the money used for the minister's salary and other church expenses. In 1949, with extensive use of congregation labor, as

East Highland Lutheran Church, rural Brandt, Deuel County, 1916 [8/18/2008]

Faith United Lutheran Church, rural Volin, Yankton County, 1916 [6/16/2010]

well as a cash fund of four thousand dollars, the church was remodeled. The Union Presbyterian Church is no longer used.[9]

EAST HIGHLAND LUTHERAN CHURCH, rural Brandt, 1916

In 1879, Rev. J. C. Jacobson lived on a farm near Volga in Brookings County. On 3 April of that year, he met in the sod home of Johannes Larson near Fish Lake (about fifteen miles southeast of Brandt) in Deuel County with others who lived in the area and organized the East Highland Lutheran Congregation. Reverend Jacobson was the pastor of the new congregation with a salary of fifty dollars per year. At the time, he also served ten other congregations in the vicinity. The Ladies' Aid Society was organized in 1887. In the first few years, members of this group often had to walk to their meetings, in some cases up to seven miles. They carried knitting and sewing to occupy their hands on these long walks. Before long, horses and buggies made these treks unnecessary.

In the summer of 1887, the congregation held a meeting at which they decided to build a church. Although the first church was enclosed in 1891, it was not completed and dedicated until 1905. The church, located one mile north and five miles east of Brandt in Norden Township, was struck by lightning and burned to the ground in August of 1914. By 1916, the church had been rebuilt and was dedicated on 30 May. It has two decorative round windows in the front, four Gothic windows on each side, and an impressive steeple. Services were held exclusively in the Norwegian language until 1937. All of the minutes of church meetings were recorded in Norwegian until 1939. A coal and wood furnace was installed in 1937; it was replaced with an oil furnace in 1954. The church was wired and electricity was brought in 1947. The structure and general appearance of the East Highland Lutheran Church has changed little during its lifetime. It is still regularly used.[10]

FAITH UNITED LUTHERAN CHURCH, rural Volin, 1916

A considerable number of people left their homes in Trondheim, Norway, between 1866 and 1868 to settle in America. Some of them settled between Clay and Turkey Creeks in Yankton County, in the northern part of Volin Township, and in all of Marindahl Township. By 1880, all of the land in that area was occupied, and most people lived in dugouts. A Reverend Nesse, from near Elk Point, held the first religious services for these people in 1870 in the home of Mr. and Mrs. Ole Bjerke. For the next two decades, services were held, sometimes by laymen and sometimes by visiting ministers, in the Marindahl School. This religious group was incorporated as the Zion Congregation on 14 December 1882.

In 1885, the Zion Congregation built a fourteen-by-eighteen-foot school on land they had acquired two miles west and three miles north of Volin in east-central Yankton County. This school was used for religious services for the next six years. In April 1891, the congregation decided to build an actual church building. The new church was twenty-eight by fifty feet, had a steeple, and cost fifteen hundred dollars to build. On 6 July 1915, lightning struck the church, burning it down. The congregation started building a new church that fall. Andrew Hall of Irene built the church, which cost fifteen thousand dollars. The new church, dedicated in October 1916, is a large wooden structure with two entrances, two steeples, a large Gothic window in the front, and a similar window on each side. It cost fifteen hundred dollars to purchase and install a pipe organ. Because of its large size and its tall steeples, the church is an impressive sight sitting by itself on the prairie.

The name of the congregation was changed to Zion Evangelical Lutheran Church on 27 February 1918. More recently, the name was changed to Faith United Lutheran Church. Originally, all the services were conducted in Norwegian, but in 1924, the minister offered English-language services every third Sunday. In 1933, two-thirds of the services were in English, and by 1942, they were entirely in English. The church is still in regular use.[11]

Saint John's Lutheran Church, Britton, Marshall County, 1917 [5/26/2010]

SAINT JOHN'S LUTHERAN CHURCH, Britton, 1917

The county seat of Marshall County, Britton is located a little west of the center of the county. The town was named after Col. Isaac Britton, one of its first residents. The German Lutheran settlers in Britton and its vicinity began holding religious services in their homes in 1889. This group recruited Rev. John Matzat to be their pastor. He soon organized the group, and on 30 October 1892, they adopted the name the German Evangelical Lutheran Congregation of Saint John's, Unaltered Augsburg Confession. The new congregation was incorporated on November 5 of the same year and simultaneously decided to build a church. Carpenter Ed Waite, who was paid one hundred fifty dollars, built the first church for the congregation. The building was twenty by twenty-eight feet with twelve-foot-high walls. From 1898 to 1902, a Reverend Octjen served the congregation. Once a month, this extraordinary man walked forty miles from his home in Waubay to instruct John, Elsa, and Rosa Muth in their catechism at their home near White Lake. He stayed overnight, and then walked to Britton to hold a service before walking the forty miles from Britton back to Waubay.

In 1900, the congregation purchased a one-manual reed organ, replacing it in 1923 with a two-manual, pedal reed organ acquired from the Methodist Church at Wyndmere, North Dakota, for $285. It took several inspection trips and much discussion to complete the deal, and today the organ is displayed at the Britton Museum. In 1916, construction began on a new church, completed and dedicated in 1917. Andrew Carlson built the building next to the original church at a cost of nine thousand dollars, including furnishings.

With the onset of World War I and the rising anti-German sentiment, pastors conducted services in English instead of German. In 1928, the church constitution was translated from German to English, and the church name was changed to Saint John's Lutheran Church. In 1935, lightning struck the steeple. The resulting fire caused smoke damage to the interior of the church, requiring complete redecoration. The church was enlarged in 1975–1976 by adding to the front of the building. This addition was dedicated on 25 April 1976. The new space houses a library, a pastor's study, and more space for Sunday school classes. This church is still in regular use. The 2010 population of Britton was 1,241.[12]

FIRST BAPTIST CHURCH, Viborg, 1917

The First Baptist Church in Viborg is in southern Turner County in the southeast part of the state. Its history, however, began in the 1860s, when many early pioneers of Danish origin began to settle in Daneville Township in Turner County and Lodi in Clay County. These people either came directly from Denmark or had previously immigrated to Wisconsin or Illinois. One of the first Protestant denominations in southeast Dakota Territory were the Baptists. The Baptists first organized a congregation in Vermillion on 16 February 1868. In 1872, a congregation formed in Lodi; in late 1872, one formed in Swan Lake Village. In late 1873, thirty-seven Danish Baptists lived in Daneville and its immediate surroundings. Some of them attended services in Lodi, quite distant by horseback or wagon, and some attended the nearer congregation in Swan Lake, only three miles north. On 31 December 1873, Rev. G. W. Freeman and thirty-three of the local Baptists organized the First Day Danish Baptist Church of Daneville at the home of Mr. and Mrs. M. L. Hoyne, about two miles east-southeast of town. For the first few years, services were held in the sod houses of members.

In 1876, a young divinity student named Nils Tychsen from the Baptist Seminary at Morgan Park, Illinois, came to Daneville to become the pastor. He quickly convinced the congregation to build their first church, which was dedicated on 14 June 1878. The two acres on which the church was built were on a hilltop one mile east and three-quarters of a mile south of Viborg and cost one dollar. In 1887, the congregation purchased ten acres of land just south of the church site and built a parsonage there. On 2 April 1889, lightning started a prairie fire that overran the Daneville community and burned down both church and parsonage. The pastor and his family narrowly escaped, although one of the parishioners was killed in the conflagration. The congregation immediately began construction of a new church in the same design as its predecessor but larger, twenty-eight by sixty-six feet.

Unfortunately for Daneville, the railroad built its tracks about a mile away, resulting in the establishment of a new town called Viborg after the Danish city of the same name. In the early 1900s, the idea of moving the Baptist church

First Baptist Church, Viborg, Turner County, 1917
[7/15/2009]

to Viborg began and steadily grew, along with the population of the new town. On 17 July 1905, the congregation placed the church on its new foundation in Viborg. The total cost of the move, including a twenty-four-by-twenty-eight-foot addition to the building, was $2,584. The relocated church was rededicated on 22 October 1905.

Viborg continued to grow during the first fifteen years of the new century, and by early 1917, a building committee was established to study a larger church. On 2 August 1917, the congregation laid the cornerstone of the new church. The Livermore and McWayne Architectural Firm of Sioux Falls developed the plans for the building in a design similar to that of the City Temple in Sioux Falls. The congregation had raised the entire cost of the new church, twenty-six hundred dollars, by the time the building was completed. The exterior of this Classic-style church is brick with a layer of Bedford limestone just below the floor line of the main level. A tall white Doric column lines either side of the front entry. The building includes a full basement, a kitchen, classrooms, and a steam-heating system. The interior trim is oak, and the curved pews face the altar, seating more than four hundred. The first service in the new church was held on 23 December 1917; it was dedicated the following January. The original church was repurposed as a parish hall for Our Savior's Lutheran Church in Viborg; the addition was used as a home.

The First Baptist Church in Viborg was the first in town to use English exclusively, although the switch from Danish was done over a fifteen-year period. By the early 1920s, all regular services were in English, with only a few special services in Danish. The early use of English helped the congregation grow because many of the new arrivals in Viborg after 1905 were not Danish. In 1919, the church sponsored the establishment of the first Boy Scout Troop in South Dakota. In 1922, the constitution of the church was amended to change the name formally to First Baptist Church of Viborg. The church is still in regular use. Viborg has a population of about 782 today.[13]

FIRST PRESBYTERIAN CHURCH, Lake Andes, 1918

The town of Lake Andes, the county seat, is located near the center of Charles Mix County in the southeast part of the state, with the Missouri River as its western border. It is on the southwest end of the eight-mile-long lake of the same name. In 2010, Lake Andes had a population of 879. Although the town of Lake Andes was not platted until 1904, white settlers were living in the area by the late 1890s. On 24 April 1898, Rev. C. M. Peck presided over a meeting in the Lake Andes School to organize a Sunday school. In June of the following year, the Sunday school spawned the initial organization of a Presbyterian church. For the first few years, services were held in area homes and schools. In 1904, the congregation acquired lots in the new town and completed a church building by the summer of 1905, dedicating

First Presbyterian Church, Lake Andes, Charles Mix County, 1918 [7/7/2008]

it in October. The church had a steeple and a six-hundred-pound bell cast by the American Bell Foundry Company of Northville, Michigan. On 10 August 1905, articles of incorporation were filed with the secretary of state for the First Presbyterian Church of Lake Andes.

Rev. Clarence Green held a series of evangelistic meetings in the City Hall in the middle 1910s, which resulted in a near doubling of the membership in the church. In the summer of 1917 the church purchased two lots in Lake Andes for two thousand dollars on which they planned to build a large Classic-style brick church. The Wold Construction Company began work on 1 May 1918. Delays in getting materials for the building because of World War I slowed completion, and it was not dedicated until 6 April 1919. The cost of the church and its furnishings was twenty thousand dollars. The church includes all stained-glass windows. During construction of the church, services were held in Central Hardware Store. In the mid-1950s the stained-glass windows were taken to Omaha for cleaning, releading, and general reconditioning. When they were reinstalled, workmen added heavy storm-glass windows to the exterior to protect the windows from deterioration. The church is still in regular use.[14]

OUR LADY OF VICTORY CHURCH, Plainview, 1918

Plainview was a small town in east-central Meade County, twenty-eight miles south and six miles west of Faith. Although Plainview was not founded until the early part of the twentieth century, it has long since disappeared. Tony Kovarik, who homesteaded near Plainview in 1908, donated land for a church and rectory in the mid-1910s, but construction did not begin until 1917. Bishop John Lawler of the Lead Diocese dedicated Our Lady of Victory Church on 23 November 1918.[15] An anonymous donor had made a five-hundred-dollar contribution toward the construction of the church, and the remaining cost was to be collected locally. A local devout Catholic, Pat Dewey, worked hard to collect that money. He owned neither a buggy nor a wagon, so he traveled around the area from farm to farm on a corn cultivator to seek donations. Pulled by two horses, a cultivator worked a single row of corn and had only a seat and a set of fixed stirrups.

Parishioners hauled the materials for the two buildings by wagon from Faith. The Catholic Extension Society also stepped forward to help with expenses. Construction of the church and rectory did not go smoothly. The first contractor absconded with the initial part of the building fund without doing any of the work. A second carpenter was hired and did a fine job with the help of donated labor from parishioners who did much of the less-skilled work on the two buildings. The first priest for the new church, Father McRory, came to Plainview from New York City, which is as opposite a place from Plainview as any could be. Because he arrived before the parsonage was built, he lived with various local

Our Lady of Victory Catholic Church, Plainview, Meade County, 1918 [7/28/2007]

Cathedral of Saint Joseph, Sioux Falls, Minnehaha County, 1919 [6/20/2006]

families for a time. One happy coincidence for Father McRory was that he loved chicken, which all the area settlers raised and used as a staple for their meals.

The rectory was sold and moved away in 1934. Members of the parish renovated the church in 1981, and, at some point, the steeple was removed. As of 2002, only seven families formed the church membership. The church is small and, with no trees or shrubs near it, appears lonely and forsaken, but services are still held there. A priest from Faith travels to conduct Mass, alternating on Saturday evenings one week and on Sunday mornings the other.[16]

CATHEDRAL OF SAINT JOSEPH, Sioux Falls, 1919

Bishop Martin Marty was appointed vicar apostolic of Dakota Territory in 1879. He chose Yankton, which at the time was the territorial capital, to be the home of the Catholic church for the territory. Sacred Heart Parish in Yankton was the first pro-cathedral church, which meant that it was not built as a cathedral but could be temporarily used as one. The territorial capital was moved to Bismarck in 1883, however, and in the following years, Sioux Falls substantially outgrew Yankton in population. In February of 1889 (the year South Dakota became a state), the diocesan headquarters were relocated to Sioux Falls, and in September of that year, Pope Leo XIII established the diocese of Sioux Falls to include the whole state.

The first Catholic parish in Sioux Falls was Saint Michael's, whose first church burned in 1881 and was replaced with a substantial brick structure. When the diocesan seat moved to Sioux Falls, Saint Michael's became the pro-cathedral. In 1896, Bishop Thomas O'Gorman succeeded Bishop Marty. During the first fifteen years of the new century, some of the larger parishes in the Sioux Falls diocese began replacing their early wooden churches with larger and more elaborate edifices. In part as a result, Bishop O'Gorman began to plan the building of a true cathedral

Interior, Cathedral of Saint Joseph [5/23/2012]

Pipe organ, Cathedral of Saint Joseph

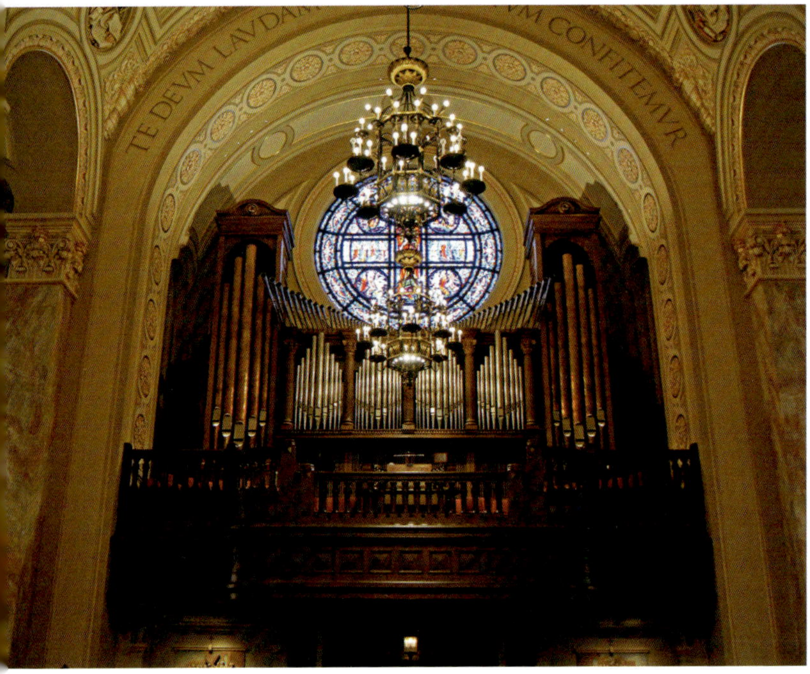

for the diocese. Early in 1915, he participated with his lifelong friend, Bishop John Ireland, in the dedication of a new cathedral in Saint Paul, Minnesota. This experience added fuel to Bishop O'Gorman's desire for a cathedral in Sioux Falls.

Bishop O'Gorman hired Emmanuel L. Masqueray, the French architect who designed the cathedral in Saint Paul, to design his dream building. The bishop and architect decided that the best site for the cathedral was the location of Saint Michael's brick church, which overlooked downtown Sioux Falls from a hillside, and that church was relocated to allow for construction of the cathedral to begin in the summer of 1915.

The state economy was doing well in 1915, which created optimism among the people of South Dakota. This optimism helped make it easier to raise money around the state for the cathedral's building fund. Masqueray passed away in May of 1917, and one of his chief assistants, Edwin Lundie of Saint Paul, was hired to complete the construction project. World War I caused other delays in the construction process, with shortages of skilled construction workers and materials, which increased expenses. The final cost was three hundred ninety thousand dollars, well above the initial bid of two hundred seventy-five thousand dollars. The building was nearly finished at the end of 1918 when the first Mass was celebrated on 8 December. The cathedral was dedicated on 7 May 1919. It is one of the largest and most impressive churches in South Dakota. Although the Romanesque exterior is somewhat stark, the interior is lavish, featuring polished columns, large stained-glass windows, paintings on the vaulted ceiling and walls, and elaborate chandeliers. The interior is reminiscent of the European Baroque cathedrals.

In 1935, a Kilgen pipe organ, donated by Monsignor Mulloney, was installed in the choir. A fire in 1942 in the lower church caused significant damage to the whole building, necessitating extensive redecoration. In 1946, the marble high altar was installed, and a year later, the original frosted glass windows were replaced with French stenciled, stained-glass windows. Early in the first decade of the new century, the cathedral underwent a large restoration project.[17]

NOTES

1. Herbert S. Schell, *History of South Dakota*, 4th ed., rev. John E. Miller (Pierre: South Dakota Historical Society Press, 2004), pp. 270–73.

2. *100 Years of Proud People, 1883–1983: A History of Sully County* (Onida, S.Dak.: Sully County Centennial Committee, 1983), pp. 174–79.

3. *The History of Lincoln County, South Dakota* (Canton, S.Dak.: Lincoln County History Committee, 1985), pp. 18, 160–62; *Canton Lutheran Church: The Story of Its Construction* (pamphlet) (Canton, S.Dak.: Canton Lutheran Church), n.d.; "The History of Augustana University," Augustana University, augie.edu.

4. Clare Miller, Irma (Greene) Thietje, and Fama L. Greene, comps., *Fedora History: Territorial Days 1985* (Fedora, S.Dak.: By the Compilers, 1985), pp. 89–91.

5. *History of Moody County* (Flandreau, S.Dak.: Moody County Historical Society, 1986), pp. 12, 17–18.

6. Jack Marken, ed., *The Making of a Community: A History of Jerauld County to 1980* (Wessington Springs, S.Dak.: Dunham Historical Society, 1982), pp. 198–200.

7. "Immanuel Dimock," Immanuel Lutheran Church, santel.net/~immanuel/history_3.html.

8. "Our History," Watertown First United Methodist Church, watertownfirstumc.com; *"The First 100 Years" in Codington County, South Dakota* (Watertown, S.Dak.: Codington County History Book Committee, 1979), pp. 3, 8.

9. Canova Centennial Committee, comp., *Pioneer Reflections: Canova, South Dakota Centennial, 1883–1983* (Canova, S.Dak., By the Compiler, 1983), pp. 60–61.

10. Deuel County History Book Committee, *Historical Collections of Deuel County* (Gary, S.Dak.: Deuel County History Book Committee, 1977), pp. 77–78.

11. Yankton County Historical Society, *History of Yankton County, South Dakota* (Dallas, Tex.: Curtis Media Corp., 1987), pp. 149-50.

12. *Britton: Centennial History, 1884–1984* (Britton, S.Dak.: Britton Journal, 1984), pp. 51–52; *Marshall County, South Dakota* (Britton, S.Dak.: Marshall County Historical Society, 1979), pp. 540–41.

13. Viborg History Book Committee, comp., *Viborg, South Dakota, 1893–1993* (Viborg, S.Dak.: By the Compilers, 1992), pp. 204–208.

14. Adeline S. Gnirk, comp. and ed., *The Epic of Papineau's Domain* (Burke, S.Dak.: By the Compiler, 1986), pp. 153–55.

15. The Catholic church had divided its single South Dakota diocese into two in 1902, one headquartered in Sioux Falls and one in Lead. The western diocese moved its seat from Lead to Rapid City in 1930. Robert F. Karolevitz, *With Faith, Hope and Tenacity: The First One Hundred Years of the Catholic Diocese of Sioux Falls, 1889–1989* (Mission Hill, S.Dak.: Dakota Homestead Publishers for the Catholic Diocese of Sioux Falls, 1989), p. 1.

16. *Faith Country Heritage, 1910–1985* (Faith, S.Dak.: Faith Historical Committee, 1985), p. 79.

17. *With Faith, Hope and Tenacity*, pp. 1, 49, 86–88, "History of the Cathedral," The Cathedral of Saint Joseph, stjosephcathedral.net.

7 : The 1920s

The 1920s were troubled times in South Dakota. World War I caused a dramatic increase in demand for many commodities, which naturally led to inflation of prices. When the war ended in 1918, that demand shrank, and prices came down. The country went from a period of inflation to one of deflation. In South Dakota, prices for farm products also fell, lowering farm income. Soon, many farmers were unable to make the payments on their debts. Real-estate values decreased 58 percent in the decade. Farm land values dropped from an average of $71 per acre in 1921 to $35 in 1930 and to $18.65 by 1935. Between 1921 and 1932, foreclosures were imposed on 34,419 South Dakota farms, comprising 19.6 percent of the farm land of the state—7,192,000 acres. An epidemic of bank failures followed: 1 in 1921, 9 in 1922, and 36 in 1923. By the end of 1924, 131 more banks had failed, and the trend continued to grow throughout the decade. Between 1920 and 1934, 71 percent of all state banks in South Dakota closed. The number in 1920 was 557; in 1934, only 148 remained. During the same span, the number of federal banks shrank from 135 to 64.[1]

During the first half of this decade, the public changed its mind concerning the state's entry into private enterprise. When asked to approve a plan to dam the Missouri River at Mobridge and build a hydroelectric plant there, the vote was roughly two-to-one against. In the same election, a law to create a state-owned bank also failed by an even larger margin. By 1924, the leaders of the Progressive Party in South Dakota had lost their political direction.[2]

The transfer of Indian lands into the hands of white farmers and land speculators continued during the 1920s; indeed, such transfers accelerated. The poverty on the reservations in the 1920s led to a comprehensive study by the Brookings Institution to determine the precise statistical social and economic condition of the Indians. The Meriam Report, published in 1928, detailed the findings, emphasizing the extreme poverty under which many of South Dakota's Indians lived. The average annual per capita individual income on the Pine Ridge Indian Reservation was $86, part of which was actually tribal income distributed to members. Another part of the yearly income came from unearned sources, such as leasing or selling of property or inheritance. The average annual per capita individual earned income at Pine Ridge was $22, or $1.83 per month. The other South Dakota reservations had slightly higher average incomes but still abysmally low. The allotment policy had been a disaster. The report helped convince President Herbert Hoover of the need for a significant reform of Indian policy. The new policy prohibited further allotments and placed all remaining surplus lands in the hands of the tribes.[3]

In spite of the difficulties of the decade, 126 churches were built in South Dakota that still stand today. Work on the Mount Rushmore sculpture began in the decade. The population growth slowed, gaining 8.8 percent, from 636,547 in 1920 to 692,849 in 1930.

FIRST PRESBYTERIAN CHURCH, Raymond, 1920

Raymond is a small town in west-central Clark County incorporated in 1909. On 31 March 1886, the Presbyterian Church of Raymond was organized by Rev. P. S. Davies and twelve new parishioners at a school. On 16 May, Rev. J. S. Butt became the pastor for the summer. He gathered subscriptions from the congregation and used that money, plus six hundred dollars he received from

First Presbyterian Church, Raymond, Clark County, 1920 [8/13/2007]

Interior, First Presbyterian Church

the Presbyterian Church in York, Pennsylvania, to build the first church. The first ordained minister was Rev. W. A. Echols, who also served as pastor of churches in Doland and Hillsdale.

The 1890s were difficult economic years for the people of Raymond and the Presbyterian church there. Many of the original settlers in the area gave up their homesteads and left. Likewise, ministers did not stay long in that decade. However, by the late 1910s, the economic situation became much better. The community and the congregation both grew. The need for a new church and the prosperity that could support it both appeared by 1919. Plans were made to build a church for eighteen thousand dollars and a manse for four thousand dollars. The inflation caused by the war resulted in actual construction costs that doubled what had been estimated. The last services in the original church were held on 4 July 1920, and the new church was dedicated on 20 July. The church has a full basement, a stucco exterior, a steep roof, and several large Romanesque stained-glass windows. Over twenty thousand dollars was raised in five-year pledges to pay for the construction. However, those good years did not last long, as the national and local economies sank in the years following the war. Many of the pledges made in the early 1920s could not be paid.

In late 1925, Rev. C. F. Geiger became the pastor. He stayed for five years and worked hard to pay off the church debt. At the time, the Derr Lumber Company was pressuring the congregation for the money owed for materials used to build the church. Reverend Geiger succeeded in getting the Presbytery to donate three thousand dollars. He also received five hundred dollars from Mrs. Dayton of Minneapolis. The Ladies Aid Society was able to secure a note to provide additional funds.

The depression continued to pressure the community and the congregation during the

1930s. They had two years without a pastor, during which time members of the parish conducted services. Rev. O. B. Oltmans became the pastor in October 1935. He quickly discovered that the property was in dire need of repairs and that a crushing portion of the debt for the church still remained. He responded positively to the challenge, and good things began to happen. The congregation worked hard to paint and repair the properties. A businessman offered to settle the church's debt for the furnace, plumbing, and some other things for twenty-five percent of what was owed. The congregation was able to raise the required amount, and that part of the debt was retired. The remaining part of the debt was a twelve-thousand-dollar loan from the National Board of Missions, on which the congregation was paying four-percent interest. Through negotiations, the board agreed to settle for less than half of the loan amount. The congregation managed to raise the necessary money, and the debt of the church was finally paid in full. The population of Raymond today is about fifty residents, and First Presbyterian Church is still in regular use.[4]

SAINT LIBORIUS CATHOLIC CHURCH, Polo, 1920

Today, the town of Polo, located in north-central Hand County, has only about ten occupied houses. It had its beginnings when a group of Catholic families settled in Fairview Township in the mid-1880s. During its early history, it was called Houdek, Kolda, and Tennis, but the residents finally settled on Polo, after the town of that name in Illinois, the origin of one of the settlers. In the early years, priests sometimes came from Orient, Zell, or Onaka to hold Mass in homes or schools. In 1904, the Catholics in Fairview Township decided to build a small church. Xavier Schaefers donated land for a church, a school, and a cemetery in what became the town of Polo. Father James Reilly supervised the construction of that first church, and the parishioners provided the labor. A priest came from Orient about eight miles north, every Sunday to hold Mass.

Saint Liborius Catholic Church, Polo, Hand County, 1920 [5/25/2012]

The parish was accepted by the Oblate Fathers of Mary Immaculate in 1920, and Father Herman Pothmann became the first resident priest. Father Pothmann had been a missionary in Mexico and in the Southwest. He convinced the congregation to build a larger church and a hall. Because of his background, the church was built in Spanish mission style. Its adobe architecture, modeled after the old missions of the Southwest and California, makes Saint Liborius unique among South Dakota churches. In 1923, the parish's parochial grade school opened in the hall, which was divided into three classrooms. Several Benedictine Sisters from Sacred Heart Convent in Yankton operated the school. The sisters also taught at the public high school across the street from the Catholic school and were partially paid by public funds. A dormitory was built to provide housing for the sisters and for boarding students.

Saint Wilfrid's Catholic Church, Woonsocket, Sanborn County, 1920 [6/17/2010]

Father Pothmann continued as parish priest until he developed cataracts and retired in 1940.

Father Cyril Poppe arrived in 1958 for a three-year term as parish priest. During that time, the boarding school was closed and the dormitories were converted into classrooms. The three original classrooms were converted back to their first form, a parish hall. The hall was then enlarged to accomodate a school gym. After sixty-five years of service, the parochial school closed in 1988. After that the Saint Liborius classrooms were rented to the public school. The church is still in regular use during the summers, served by a priest from Orient.[5]

SAINT WILFRID'S CATHOLIC CHURCH, Woonsocket, 1920

Woonsocket was founded in 1883 as a siding on the Chicago, Milwaukee, & Saint Paul Railroad line through Sanborn County. The superintendent of the railroad was C. H. Prior, who named the town after his hometown of Woonsocket, Rhode Island. The town surrounds a small but attractive man-made lake, named Lake Prior after the superintendent. Soon after the founding of Woonsocket, Cornelius Carr bought the second lot sold in town and built a furniture store. The second floor of the store served as his home, where the first Catholic Mass in Woonsocket was conducted by Father J. C. Ahern, who lived on his homestead in Diana Township, about seventeen miles east of Woonsocket. Father Ahern, a circuit-rider who served Catholics all over Sanborn County, continued to hold services in the Carr home once a month until the congregation outgrew that space. For a time after that, Mass was held in the Weir School.

Parishioners purchased lots from the Townsite Company for a church, allowing them to pay half the amount normally charged. In 1884, a carpenter named Docter supervised the construction of a frame building, with most of the work done by parishioners. The wood frame, forty-by-sixty-foot structure cost fifteen hundred dollars to build. Around the turn of the century, when the congregation outgrew the capacity of the church, it was doubled in size. A furnace was installed at that time. In the early 1900s, four Presentation nuns taught Catholic school in a house. In 1904, lots were purchased for a school and a cemetery. Saint Joseph's School opened in September 1910, offering complete primary and secondary courses of education.

In the early 1910s, the congregation again became too large for the church building, prompting new planning. A Minneapolis architect designed the new edifice. A member of the parish, L. G. Turgeon, was given the construction contract, and work began on 14 May 1914. Then World War I intervened in the process. At that

Saint Joseph's Catholic Church, Mud Butte, Meade County, 1921 [5/26/2012]

time, four Eudist priests of a French order from Canada served the parish, and three of them were required to return to France to serve military duty. Although the cornerstone had been laid in October 1915, work on the church stopped soon thereafter and would not resume for nearly three years. The building was finally completed in 1920 and was dedicated on June 13 of that year. It is a large brick structure with an imposing tower at the front. Small stone mosaics by Conrad Schmidt and Company serve as interior decorations. During the 1920s, the parish hall was used for public events to raise money to pay the debts of the congregation. Frequently, Lawrence Welk, who was serving as the station band for radio station WNAX in Yankton, brought his band to the hall. In 1952, the church underwent redecoration, and the mosaics were cleaned. In 1968, the parish was notified that the Presentation Order would no longer be able to supply the nuns to staff Saint Joseph's School, which resulted in its closing. The school building was subsequently purchased by the Woonsocket School District. The church is still in regular use, and in 2011, the parish began a massive restoration project to stabilize the structure.[6]

SAINT JOSEPH'S CATHOLIC CHURCH, Mud Butte, 1921

At 3,482 square miles, Meade County is the largest in the state, nearly as large as Rhode Island and Delaware together. It is also one of the most remote and unpopulated counties in South Dakota. It was named after the army fort, Fort Meade, near Sturgis, established in 1878. The fort was named for General George Meade. Mud Butte is in the northwest corner of the county, about thirty-five miles northeast of Newell. It was never a legitimate town. There has always been a general store, named the Mud Butte Store, but never much more than that. It is now unincorporated and has only several houses. The town is named for the butte that is a few miles to the west. In May of 1910, the Mud Butte Post Office was established in the home of an early settler, Martin Mahoney, near the butte of the same name.

Jack McDermott was another early settler. His homestead was about four miles east of Mud Butte. Being a good Catholic, McDermott wanted a church nearby and conveyed that desire to the bishop. He also donated property on which such a church could be built. In the fall of 1921, priest Father Thomas Healy, who lived thirty miles south of Mud Butte in Fairpoint, and some parishioners did most of the work to build a church about two miles from Mud Butte. Carpenter Albert Schuelke directed the construction. Father Healy drove to and from Mud Butte in a Model T Ford and said Mass in the homes of Jack McDermott and Jim Fox until the church was built. It was not dedicated until June 1922.

In 1946, the church was moved about two miles and now is about one-quarter mile south of the Mud Butte Store. Saint Joseph's Church was always a mission, meaning it never had its own priest. Through its lifetime, it has been served by several different parishes, such as those in Newell, Fairpoint, and Red Owl. The church is still in regular use.[7]

SAINT ANTHONY OF PADUA CATHOLIC CHURCH, Hoven, 1921

Hoven is a small town in northwest Potter County in the north-central part of the state. Its population in 2010 was 406. In the early 1880s, the few Catholics there were visited only twice a year by a priest. However, these people met regularly to read Scripture and say the rosary. Although the first settlers came from a variety of places, among the main wave of immigrants was a significant number of German-Russians, many of whom had first settled in states east and south of South Dakota. Out of concern for these German-speaking people, Bishop Thomas O'Gorman sought a German-speaking priest to serve the area. He chose Father Anthony Helmbrecht, who had emigrated from Bavaria and previously served in New York City and Milwaukee. Father Helmbrecht became the pastor of the first Catholic church in Hoven, named Saint Bernard's, in 1908.

Soon after his arrival in Hoven, Father Helmbrecht began efforts to convince the parishioners to build a school. His initial idea was to spend fifteen thousand dollars on the new building, a figure that caused great anxiety among the congregation. However, construction began on the three-story school in September 1908, and it was completed a year later. Because of the persuasive powers of Father Helmbrecht, the school, at a final cost of twenty-seven thousand dollars, was nearly paid for before it was used. It was the first Catholic school in the state. Quite naturally, Father Helmbrecht earned widespread respect for managing to establish the school.

Father Helmbrecht next turned his building ambitions toward replacing the original church, which had been damaged by a storm and needed major repairs. In addition, the congregation had grown too large for it. Father Helmbrecht was not interested in just replacing the building with a larger frame church. He had much higher aspirations, and he was confident that he could convince the congregation to make the necessary sacrifices to support a monumental edifice as their place of worship. In 1911, he traveled to Milwaukee to meet with architect Anton Dohmen.

Dohmen, who was born in Bavaria in 1861, immigrated to the United States in 1892 after studying architecture in Germany. He settled in Milwaukee, worked with other architects for a time, and then started his own business designing churches, schools, hospitals, commercial buildings, and homes. From 1900 to 1922, he designed nineteen churches in the Midwest and Northern Great Plains. As a transplanted European whose clients were also immigrants from Europe, Dohmen naturally looked to churches of his home country for inspiration. Like many of the churches built in Europe after AD 1100, his were usually Romanesque, Gothic, or mixtures of the two styles.

After meeting with Dohmen, Father Helmbrecht immediately went about the business of raising funds to build a large impressive church in Hoven. He visited each parish family to solicit money. He had a mammoth task before him: the estimated cost of his church was two hundred twenty-five thousand dollars. Although the first half of the decade after 1910 was not a good time for farmers, Father Helmbrecht was successful in raising the money. He demonstrated his own commitment to the project by donating his entire salary for one year. He decided to build the church in two stages. First, they would build a roofed basement and hold services there until they had the money to build the church itself.

Saint Anthony of Padua Catholic Church, Hoven, Potter County, 1921 [5/25/2010]

Parishioners dug the basement using an excavator machine pulled by sixteen horses. Area farmers hauled more than a thousand wagonloads of gravel, sand, and stone to the church site for the foundation. By Christmas 1912, the basement was nearly completed, and the first Mass was said there. A sequence of poor crop years followed, and the parish made little progress in collecting the funds to build the church. In 1917, after the farm economy had improved, Father Helmbrecht resumed his construction collections among the two hundred families of the congregation. By late 1919, he proudly announced that the church would soon be built. He returned to visit Dohmen in Milwaukee and returned with the plans for a large Romanesque-style building, modeled after a larger thousand-year-old cathedral that stood in Ruhmannsfelden, Bavaria. The building was to be 160 by 64 feet and have two towers at the front that rose 130 feet into the air. The parish hired Anton Zwack of Dubuque, Iowa, the skilled contractor who had recently built a Dohmen-designed church in Strasburg, North Dakota, for the construction.

The church was enclosed, and the first Mass was celebrated there on Easter 1921. The construction was completed in early 1922. Such a massive monument in such a small prairie town was naturally an instant tourist attraction. The towers were visible from miles away from all directions. Three bells weighing a total of two tons were installed in the towers. The sheer size of the edifice was remarkable. It seated twelve hundred people, more than twice the population of the town at the time. The large altar is so heavy it is supported by a five-by-eight-foot column of concrete that begins on the floor of the basement. The vaulted ceiling is forty-six feet above the floor. The two rows of columns that support the vaulted ceiling are made of plaster painted to resemble marble and are topped with Corinthian capitals. Karl Riemann designed the thirty-one stained-glass windows that depict a wide variety of scenes from the life of Christ and the saints. The whole interior of the church is decorated in subtle colors and less garishly than some Baroque-style buildings. The fourteen Stations of the Cross hanging on the side walls are painted, three-dimensional, bas-relief sculptures. Each of these is four by five feet.

The church was dedicated on the twenty-fifth anniversary of Father Hambrecht's ordination, 30 May 1923. The total cost of the church was $215,497, and just one year after it was completed, only about twenty-five thousand dollars of the

Saint Anthony of Padua Catholic Church [5/19/2008]

Interior, Saint Anthony of Padua Catholic Church

debt remained. The parish changed its name from Saint Bernard's to Saint Anthony of Padua, in honor of their beloved priest, Father Anthony Helmbrecht. A massive seventeen-rank pipe organ with 1,127 pipes was installed in the balcony in 1930.

By the early 1980s, the church was showing the effects of sixty years of the Northern Great Plains climate. All those years of using a coal furnace, as well as the burning of countless candles, had left the interior paint faded and dirty. In places, the plaster was beginning to crumble and the paint was peeling. The roof had begun to leak. Some pieces of stained glass had migrated away from the lead seams. Three windows were stuck open. Contractors were asked for advice on the necessary repairs and restoration. Only one gave an estimate—five hundred thousand dollars—and even that number was not guaranteed. The parish priest, Father Edward Burian, met with the congregation leaders and suggested that the parishioners do the restoration. This shocking proposition seemed unrealistic, given the interior dimensions of Saint Anthony of Padua Church.

After hearing the priest's recommendation, however, one elderly member of the congregation, William Rausch, spent the entire night designing a movable scaffold from which workers could reach the ceiling and high parts of the walls. This large wooden device was subsequently built inside the church. It was twenty-two feet tall and had a railing around the top to prevent accidental falls. The structure was large enough that workers could get to about one-quarter of the ceiling without moving it. Workers climbed onto the scaffold from the balcony. To reach the highest parts of the vaulting, they placed ladders and additional smaller scaffolding on top of the large scaffold, which stayed in the nave for five years until the work was completed. The fundraising goal of one hundred twenty thousand dollars was established. In response, the congregation raised two hundred sixteen thousand dollars.

The workers scrubbed virtually every square inch of the interior of the church with an industrial cleaning liquid. All of the elaborate decorations were repainted with custom-mixed paint to match the original colors. The repeating

Saint Charles Borromeo Catholic Church, Saint Francis, Todd County, 1922 [8/16/2005]

patterns on the walls and ceiling were originally created with stencils. Workers created new stencils, using scalpels, to guide in repainting those designs. They used sponges to paint, followed by the application of varnish. They repaired and repainted plaster statues. The parish had to search nationally to find the quantity of gold-leaf paint needed for the decorations. One of the few jobs done commercially was repairs of the exterior of the towers, for which a tall crane was brought to Hoven. More than twenty thousand man-hours of donated labor were expended in the repair effort. The church remains a great monument on the prairie and the foremost tourist attraction of the region. Saint Anthony's is often called the Cathedral of the Prairies.[8]

SAINT CHARLES BORROMEO CATHOLIC CHURCH, Saint Francis, 1922

In the early 1870s, the government assigned religious denominations to individual reservations to administer the agencies and educate the Indians. The Catholic church was largely left out of this process, possibly because several members of President Ulysses S. Grant's administration were Masons. However, some of the Teton Sioux had had contact with an early missionary, Father Pierre-Jean De Smet, a Jesuit priest who was born and educated in Belgium, and he had impressed them favorably. As a result, Chief Spotted Tail of the Rosebud Agency and Chief Red Cloud of the Pine Ridge Agency traveled to Washington in September of 1877 and met with President Rutherford B. Hayes to ask him to send Jesuit clergymen, whom they called Black Robes, to their reservations to educate their people. However, it did not happen quickly. After the death of Spotted Tail in 1881, Chief Two Strike of Rosebud directly invited the Jesuits to come to the reservation and establish a school. In response, Father Jutz and Brother Nunlist went to the Rosebud Agency and, with the help of a large donation from Mother Katherine Drexel, a rich nun from Philadelphia who later became a saint, built a forty-by-ninety-five-foot frame church in 1885 at the future site of the town of Saint Francis. Brother Henry Wissing served as architect and construction supervisor for the church, which they named Saint Charles Borromeo.

Father Florentine Digmann arrived at this mission in 1888. He brought with him three Franciscan nuns, Sisters Kostka, Rosalia, and Alcantara. These three established the Saint Francis of Assisi Mission School near Saint Charles Borromeo Church. Father Digmann

Interior, Saint Charles Borromeo Catholic Church

went on to create thirty-seven mission stations around the reservation. Because many of the people on the reservation eventually moved to towns, the church gradually closed these missions, and most have disappeared. Only six parishes now serve the reservation. On 20 January 1916, the church and many of the mission buildings burned down.

The following year, the parishioners, led by Brother Andrew Hartman, began building a new church. To guard against another fire, he and his workers constructed the new building with eighteen-inch-thick concrete walls. The church, decorated with Sioux motifs, was completed and dedicated in 1922. In the early years of the twenty-first century, the church underwent renovation. The whole interior was redecorated. Artist George Hatcher accomplished this painstaking task. The twenty-four stained-glass windows were completely re-leaded. The exterior of the church is distinguished by its purple color.[9]

CHAPEL OF THE HOLY SPIRIT (EPISCOPAL), rural Firesteel, 1923

Firesteel is in the northwest part of Dewey County on the Cheyenne River Indian Reservation (near its northern border). The town, established in 1910, was named after the nearby Firesteel Creek. In the late 1880s, Episcopalian missionaries built a small one-story wooden building as a preaching station along Firesteel Creek in Corson County on the southern border of Standing Rock, about ten miles north-northwest of Firesteel. As the wooden structure aged, the Indian congregation worked to put money aside for a new church.

In 1922, a surprise bequest made a new building possible sooner than expected. Mrs. George Cabot Ward of New York, a lifelong friend of Episcopal Bishop William Hobart Hare, had financially supported his missionary work in the Northern Great Plains, in particular the building of churches on the reservations. The Society of the Double Temple in New York, which was also involved in philanthropy for the Indians of the Northern Great Plains, wanted to create a memorial to Mrs. Ward in South Dakota to recognize her many donations. They decided to build two memorial chapels in South Dakota. The northern chapel was to be built at the site of the preaching station on Firesteel Creek. The Society contributed the balance necessary to build the new church in Mrs. Ward's honor. Alfred Merton Githens, a New York architect, designed the architectural plans for the chapel for no fee. Friends of Mrs. Ward contributed the furnishings, altar books, a bell, and a communion service.

Construction began in the summer of 1922. Frank Waggoner of Keldron, a town in the northwest corner of the Standing Rock reservation, directed the construction of the chapel. Waggoner was a stonemason and building

Chapel of the Holy Spirit (Episcopal), rural Firesteel, Corson County, 1923 [8/18/2005]

Interior, Chapel of the Holy Spirit

contractor. In 1890, he had built the coffin for Sitting Bull. His wife, Josephine McCarthy Waggoner, was a member of the Standing Rock Sioux Tribe. Waggoner managed a crew of Indian volunteers, who quarried blue-gray sandstone blocks from a ridge above the site of the chapel. The blocks were rolled down the hill as far as they would go on their own. They were then loaded onto a stone boat (a flat sled without wheels), which a team of horses pulled to the construction site. Waggoner, with the help of volunteers, finished the rough stones there before they were placed on the walls of the building. The chapel was dedicated on 5 June 1923. The local people refer to it as the Old Stone Church. Two of the distinguishing features of the chapel are the large stone arch over the altar and the seven-foot-high Niobrara Cross embedded in the front wall above the doorway. Bishop Hare designed the Niobrara Cross in 1874, and small versions were given to Indians when they were confirmed to Christianity. The walls of the chapel are eighteen to twenty inches thick.

By 2000, the chapel needed serious restoration. For this project, the Mary Chilton Daughters of the Revolution Foundation donated seventy-five hundred dollars; the Deadwood Historic Preservation Fund donated ten thousand dollars; the descendants of Frank and Josephine Waggoner made a significant donation; an anonymous donor contributed ten thousand dollars; and numerous smaller donations were received. The two primary parts of the restoration were the complete replacement of the roof and the tuck pointing (removing and replacing mortar) of the stonework. Currently, the chapel is accessible only by several miles of travel through a private ranch. It was listed in the National Register of Historic Places in 1996. The chapel sometimes is used for special events, such as weddings.[10]

United Methodist Church, Geddes, Charles Mix County, 1925 [7/7/2008]

UNITED METHODIST CHURCH, Geddes, 1925

The town of Geddes lies near the center of Charles Mix County, the boundaries of which east and south of Geddes are within the Yankton Indian Reservation. The reservation was opened to limited settlement in 1879. Initially, the homesteaders were white men who had married into the tribe. Rev. T. J. Davis, pastor of a Methodist congregation in Edgerton, ten miles northwest, presented the first sermon in Geddes from a lumber wagon on Main Street on 29 April 1900. Reverend Davis moved the Edgerton church and parsonage to Geddes during the following summer, and it became the Geddes Methodist Episcopal Church. In the beginning, Reverend Davis preached in a canvas tent, making plans to build a church. Contractor A. W. Chaffee began construction in the spring of 1901 and completed the building in 1902.

At the end of World War I, the Congregational church in Geddes lost its pastor, and in 1921, it merged with the Methodist Episcopal group. The new church was named the Geddes Community Methodist Church, and it met in the Congregational church that had been built in 1901. A fire caused by an overheated stove burned down this Methodist church on Christmas morning 1921. Until a new structure could be built, services were held in the building that had been the Congregational church.

Construction began in 1924 on a new brick church. The cornerstone was laid on 5 April 1925, and the building was dedicated on 9 August 1925. The new church, large for such a small town, cost forty thousand dollars to build. The drought and depression that began in 1929 lasted through most of the 1930s. Making the payments on the construction debt became a serious problem. In response, Rev. L. J. Sheldon created the so-called pig club, in which each congregation member pledged the price of a marketable pig each year until the debt was retired. If the member had a pig, the pig was sold and the proceeds given to the church. Those who did not have a pig donated the value of a pig. This strategy eventually lowered the debt to six thousand dollars. The Board of Home Missions lent this amount to the congregation at a low interest rate. Finally, in 1944, after nineteen years, the church was debt free. In 1947, the church underwent some significant repairs and refurbishing. The roof was rebuilt; the heating equipment was reconditioned; and the entire interior was repainted and redecorated. The church, whose name is now United Methodist Church, is still in regular use. In 2010, the population of Geddes was 208.[11]

FIRST PRESBYTERIAN CHURCH, Aberdeen, 1927

Aberdeen, initially called Sod Town, began when the railroad tracks from Minneapolis reached the site. Soon after the first settlers began to build homes and live in Aberdeen, they held

First Presbyterian Church, Aberdeen, Brown County, 1927 [8/15/2007]

Sunday school meetings but only had services when a minister could be found. On 1 May 1881, a horseback Presbyterian missionary, Rev. H. B. Johnson, came to Aberdeen from Watertown and preached his first sermon in the Sod Hotel. He returned to Aberdeen the first Sunday in June to hold services again, this time in a partially built store. He persuaded a political leader of Aberdeen, who was a Baptist, to circulate a petition for the organization of a Presbyterian congregation. Three Presbyterians and three other citizens signed the petition. In January 1882, eleven members meeting again in a store officially organized the congregation. Reverend Johnson convinced them to build a church and the Church Extension Society of the National Presbyterian church to donate five hundred dollars for its construction.

Lots were donated to the new congregation, and a church was built that year, the first church in Aberdeen. This building was not heated, and when the weather was seriously cold, Reverend Johnson preached wearing his overcoat, gloves, and a cap with the earflaps down. In 1882 and 1883, services were not held in January because of the bitter cold. During the early years, the congregation rented the church to the Methodists for their services every other week for $1.25 a Sunday. In 1896, the congregation built its second church and sold the first one to the Zion Lutheran Congregation.

The early Presbyterians of Aberdeen were principled and strict people. They led a movement for woman suffrage and practiced what they preached. In 1890, they elected two women to their board of deacons. The congregation expelled two members for being dishonest businessmen. They also strictly outlawed social gatherings in the church. They even discouraged card playing by their members.

In 1926 and 1927 a large, brick, English Gothic-style church was built. The architect was George Fossum, who lived in Aberdeen. The front of the church is asymmetric, having a short but wide tower on its left side and no tower on its right side. A huge Gothic stained-glass window with elaborate tracing looms over the entry. Similar but smaller windows appear on the sides and front. The bell in the present church came for the first church and was also used in the second one. Church membership at the time of the new construction was over six hundred fifty. The church is still in regular use.[12]

OUR SAVIOR'S LUTHERAN CHURCH, rural Firesteel, 1927

Settlers, primarily Scandinavians, began to settle north of Firesteel in 1910 and were soon requesting ministers. In June of 1911, a student from the Lutheran Free Church spent a week preaching in the area. Later that summer, Rev. R. O. Aase from Mobridge held services around Firesteel. The following summer, ministers came by train from Mobridge to hold services in homes and a tent. In 1913, Reverend Lee came to Firesteel from North Dakota to help organize

Our Savior's Lutheran Church, rural Firesteel, Dewey County, 1927 [8/19/2005]

Our Savior's Lutheran Church, which initially had thirty-one charter members.

Henry Olson, a remarkable man, taught the first Sunday school in the congregation. Being a talented musician and singer, Olson also served as pianist, a member of the quartet, and the choir director for the church. He gave piano and violin lessons and organized a band. He even made violins. Finally, he served as the chief carpenter when the congregation built its brick church in the mid-1920s on land three miles north and one and one-half miles east of Firesteel, just south of the county line between Dewey and Corson counties. The construction was financed with a loan of one thousand dollars, and parishioners provided the labor. Horse teams pulling slips dug the basement. The needed sand was hauled by wagon from the Grand River about fifteen miles north of the church site.

Our Savior's Lutheran Church was completed in 1927. It had three Gothic windows and four small buttresses on each side, as well as a steeple. At the rear of the church is a five-sided extension to provide the space where the minister conducted services. By the early 1960s many of the former rural residents of the area had moved to towns, prompting the building of a new Lutheran church in Timber Lake. For a time, both churches were used, but in 1974, Our Savior's Lutheran Church was abandoned.[13]

UNITED METHODIST CHURCH, Gettysburg, 1927

Platted in 1884, Gettysburg is the county seat of Potter County. It was named after the Civil War battlefield in Pennsylvania because many of the first settlers had fought in that battle. The first Methodist services in Gettysburg were held by

United Methodist Church, Gettysburg, Potter County, 1927 [5/19/2008]

the circuit rider Rev. O. H. Sprohl, who organized the Methodist church there in July 1884. In the first years of the congregation, services were held on the second floor of the Branshaw Building, which served as a classroom on weekdays. Sometimes services were held in the dance pavilion built for the Fourth of July celebration. After the Baptist church was built, the Methodists used that building for one service each Sunday. The congregation also met with other local denominations in an integrated Sunday school.

In 1890, the Methodist congregation built their first church. Unfortunately, the building did not last long; a tornado destroyed it in 1892. Services were held for a while in the Episcopal church and then in space rented on the second floor of the O'Neill Building. Next, the congregation rented the Baptist church, the W. R. C. Hall, and then the Congregational church. Finally, in 1910–1911, they built a second, larger church. This fine large brick structure had stained-glass windows and a tower with a battlemented top. It was dedicated on 10 March 1912. The Ladies Aid Society had raised funds for this building through food sales, socials, dinners, and bazaars.

The second church lasted longer than the first, but only thirteen years after dedication, it burned down on 18 November 1925. Almost immediately, the congregation began building the third church, a large rectangular brick structure that was dedicated in 1927. Once again, the Ladies Aid Society actively participated in fundraising, serving breakfasts, lunches, and banquets for organizations such as the Kiwanis and Rotary. They also sold cosmetics, homemade quilts, comforters, rugs, original sheet music, and cookbooks with local recipes. And they held food sales and bazaars.

The church does not have the appearance of a traditional church. With the exceptions of two round windows on the front and a large window on each side, it looks more like a civic building than a church. It has no steeple or tower. The mortgage on this building was burned in a ceremony on 30 September 1945. The parsonage was built and dedicated in 1949. The name of the church was changed to United Methodist Church in 1968, after the Methodists merged with the Evangelical United Brethren Church. In 2010, the population of Gettysburg was 1,162.[14]

NOTES

1. Herbert S. Schell, *History of South Dakota*, 4th ed., rev. John E. Miller (Pierre: South Dakota Historical Society Press, 2004), pp. 283–84. A personal anecdote demonstrates this crisis. One day in 1924, my grandfather, Louis Sebesta, was in Kimball to pay his real-estate taxes at the bank. Afterward, he decided on a whim to buy a new Dodge touring car and paid for it with a check. The car dealer, Charlie Havlik, quickly crossed the street to the bank and cashed the check. Shortly after that, the bank closed and never reopened. Havlik had gotten the last cash to leave the bank. If Grandpa had not used money from his bank account on the car that day, it would have been lost to him. Our family always called that Dodge their "free" car.

2. Ibid., p. 275.

3. Shell, *History of South Dakota*, p. 312–13; R. Alton Lee, *A New Deal for South Dakota: Drought, Depression, and Relief, 1920–1941* (Pierre: South Dakota Historical Society Press, 2016), p. 125.

4. *Centennial History of the Northern Two-Thirds of Clark County* (Garden City, S.Dak.: Clark County Historical Society, 1981), pp. 233–34.

5. Scott Heidepriem, *Bring on the Pioneers!: History of Hand County* (Miller, S.Dak.: By the Author, 1978), pp. 105–6; Robert F. Karolevitz, *With Faith, Hope and Tenacity: The First One Hundred Years of the Catholic Diocese of Sioux Falls, 1889–1989* (Mission Hill, S.Dak.: Dakota Homestead Publishers for the Catholic Diocese of Sioux Falls, 1989), pp. 154–55.

6. Charles Woodard, ed., *Reminiscing: A Centennial History of Sanborn County and Woonsocket* (Minneapolis, Minn.: Josten Publications, 1983), pp. 27, 30–31, 73–76; "History," St. Wilfrid's Catholic Church, santel.net/~stwilfrid.

7. *Faith Country Heritage, 1910–1985* (Faith, S.Dak.: Faith Historical Committee, 1985), pp. 1, 81, 200–201.

8. James Coomber and Sheldon Green, *Magnificent Churches on the Prairie* (Fargo: North Dakota Institute for Regional Studies, 1997), pp. 15–16, 60–71; Jerry Wilson, "The Little Town with the Big Church," in *South Dakota's Best Stories*, ed. Bernie Hunhoff (Yankton, S.Dak.: Middle Border Books, 2004), pp. 155–56. For more on Dohmen and the churches he designed on the prairies, *see* James E. Coomber, Denis R. Fournier, and Sheldon W. Green, "Building Churches on the Prairie: The Partnership of Bishop Vincent Wehrle and Anton Dohmen," *North Dakota History* 65 (Winter 1998): 17–26.

9. "Mission History" and "St. Charles Borromeo Parish," St. Francis Mission among the Lakota, sfmission.org; Francis Paul Prucha, *The Great Father: The United States Government and the American Indians*, 2 vols. (Lincoln: University of Nebraska Press, 1984), 1:512, 516–19.

10. Jack Bickel, "Holy Spirit Chapel: 'The Old Stone Church'" and "Restoration Gave Chapel New Life," in *Timber Lake and Area Centennial History, 1910–2010* (Timber Lake, S.Dak.: Timber Lake and Area Historical Society, 2009), pp. 168–72.

11. Adeline S. Gnirk, comp., *Epic of Papineau's Domain* (Burke, S.Dak.: By the Compiler, 1986), pp. 96–97.

12. Brown County Museum and Historical Society, [comp.], *Brown County History* (Aberdeen, S.Dak.: North Plains Press, 1980), pp. 236–37; "Our History," First Presbyterian Church, Aberdeen, firstpresbyterianchurchaberdeen.com.

13. Helen Pederson, "Our Savior's Lutheran Church–Firesteel," in *Timber Lake and Area, 1910–1985*, ed. Ginny Cudmore and Jim Nelson (Timber Lake, S.Dak.: Timber Lake and Area Historical Society, 1984), pp. 221–23.

14. Cece and Ruth Stilgeboner, comps., *Gettysburg, South Dakota: 75th Anniversary, July 11–12, 1958* (Gettysburg, S.Dak.: Diamond Jubilee Committee, 1958), pp. 10, 64; Potter County Historical Association, comp., *Potter County: People, Pictures and Progress, 1883–1983* (Gettysburg, S.Dak.: By the Compiler, 1983), pp. 301–3.

8 : Lasting Legacy, 1870–1929

Photographic Record of Surviving Churches Built before 1930

AURORA COUNTY

Underwood United Methodist Church, 11 miles north of White Lake, 1908 [7/8/2008]

Saint Paul's Lutheran Church, Plankinton, 1913, not used as a church since 1962 [8/10/2006]

Aurora Reformed Church, Aurora Center, 1913 [7/8/2008]

Saint Mary's Catholic Church, Stickney, 1910 [6/16/2010]

Saint John Lutheran Church, Stickney, 1920 (Presbyterian church until 1945) [7/8/2008]

Saint John's Catholic Church, Plankinton, 1923 [8/10/2006]

Storla Lutheran Church, Storla, 1928 [8/10/2006]

BEADLE COUNTY

Immanuel Lutheran Church, 9 miles south, 5 miles east of Iroquois, 1883 [8/10/2006]

Broadland United Methodist Church, Broadland, 1883 [7/9/2008]

First Presbyterian Church, Huron, 1910 [7/9/2008]

Bonilla Presbyterian Church, Bonilla, 1916 [7/9/2008]

Virgil Methodist Episcopal Church, Virgil, 1918 [7/9/2008]

Congregational United Church of Christ, Huron, 1919 [7/9/2008]

American Lutheran Church, Huron, 1926 [6/17/2010]

Unknown church, Cavour, date unknown [7/9/2008]

Unknown church, Hitchcock, date unknown [8/13/2007]

Concordia Lutheran Church, Wessington, date unknown (originally Peace Lutheran in Virgil) [7/9/2008]

BENNETT COUNTY

Community Presbyterian Church, Tuthill, 1926 [6/14/2010]

First Body of Jesus Christ Church, Batesland, 1927 [6/14/2010]

BON HOMME COUNTY

First Presbyterian Church, Scotland, 1881, enlarged 1915 [6/8/2006]

United Methodist Church, Scotland, 1884 [6/8/2006]

Wesleyan Church, Avon, 1885 (moved into town in 1901), now a museum [7/14/2009]

Bon Homme Memorial Church, Tyndall, 1885, now a museum [6/24/2006]

Saint Andrew's Episcopal Church, Scotland, 1888 [6/8/2006]

Tyndall Baptist Church, Tyndall, 1905 (Congregational until 1929) [6/8/2006]

Bethlehem Lutheran Church, Perkins, 1894 (Congregational until bought by Lutherans in 1942), used until 1963 [5/22/2012]

Saint Wenceslaus Catholic Church, Tabor, 1899 [5/25/2006]

United Methodist Church, Tyndall, 1905 (originally First Methodist Episcopal Church) [8/7/2006]

Tyndall Presbyterian Church, Tyndall, 1914 [7/14/2009]

First Presbyterian Church, Avon, 1917 [6/7/2006]

United Church of Christ, Springfield, 1921 [7/14/2009]

Fellowship Baptist Church, Scotland, 1929 (originally Bethany Reformed) [6/8/2006]

BROOKINGS COUNTY

First United Presbyterian Church, Brookings, 1886 [8/17/2008]

United Parish of Elkton, Elkton, 1888 (Methodist until 1967) [8/17/2008]

Lake Campbell Lutheran Church, 8 miles south, 2 miles east of Volga, 1890 [8/17/2008]

Oslo Lutheran Church, Volga, 1892 [5/19/2009]

First Baptist Church, White, 1893 (German Methodist until 1920) [5/19/2009]

Zion Lutheran Church, White, 1897 [5/19/2009]

United Methodist Church, Bruce, 1897 [5/19/2009]

First United Methodist Church, Brookings, 1904 [8/17/2008]

Olivet Presbyterian Church, Volga, 1916 [5/28/2010]

Saint Paul's Catholic Church, White, 1898 [5/19/2009]

Saint William's Catholic Church, Aurora, 1910 [5/19/2009]

Saint Paul's Episcopal Church, Brookings, 1917 [7/16/2009]

First Baptist Church, Brookings, 1918 [8/17/2008]

Singsass Lutheran Church, 3 miles south, 1 mile east of Astoria, 1921 [9/9/2013]

First English Lutheran Church, Aurora, 1923 [5/19/2009]

BROWN COUNTY

Finnish Apostolic Lutheran Church, 5.5 miles east, 6 miles north of Frederick, 1884 [8/15/2007]

Trinity Episcopal Church, Groton, 1884 [5/21/2009]

United Methodist Church, Frederick, 1886 [5/26/2010]

United Methodist Church, Bath, 1887 (moved from Putney in 1944) [8/15/2007]

Claremont Methodist Church, Claremont, 1888 [8/15/2007]

B'Nai Isaac Synagogue, Aberdeen, 1890 (Aberdeen Wesleyan until 1917) [5/25/2012]

Scandinavia Lutheran Church, 1 mile west, 3 miles north of Stratford, 1896 [5/21/2009]

Aurland United Norwegian Lutheran Church, 4.5 miles east, 5 miles south of Frederick, 1897 [8/15/2007]

Augustana Lutheran Church, 4.5 miles south, 1 mile east of Claremont, 1899 (originally Swedish Evangelical Lutheran) [7/18/2007]

First Presbyterian Church, Mansfield, 1905 [7/16/2009]

Saint Paul's Lutheran Church, Stratford, 1908 [7/16/2009]

Hecla United Methodist Church, Hecla, 1900 [8/15/2007]

Groton Christian and Missionary Alliance Church, Groton, 1907 [5/21/2009]

Stratford Presbyterian Church, Stratford, 1909, abandoned 1997 [7/16/2009]

First United Methodist Church, Aberdeen, 1909 [8/15/2007]

Congregational Christian Church, Colombia, 1910 (moved from Claremont in 1947) [8/15/2007]

First Presbyterian Church, Groton, 1911 [8/14/2007]

Sacred Heart Catholic Church, Westport, 1914 [7/16/2009]

Calvary Chapel Community Church, Aberdeen, 1918 (Aberdeen Wesleyan until 1918) [8/15/2007]

Saint John's Evangelical Lutheran Church, Colombia, 1918 [8/15/2007]

Savo Evangelical Lutheran Church, 4.5 miles east, 3 miles north of Frederick, 1922 [8/15/2007]

Saint Paul's Lutheran Church, Frederick, 1923 [5/26/2010]

Trinity Lutheran Church, Houghton, 1926 (originally Norwegian Lutheran) [8/15/2007]

Faith United Methodist Church, Aberdeen, 1927 (originally First Evangelical Church) [8/15/2007]

First Presbyterian Church, Aberdeen, 1927 [8/15/2007]

BRULE COUNTY

Holy Trinity Catholic Church, Kimball, 1893 (moved from Bendon), now a museum [6/18/2010]

Christ Episcopal Church, Chamberlain, 1894 [6/26/2009]

Saint Procopious Catholic Church, 10 miles south of Pukwana, 1895 [8/5/2005]

Interior, Saint Procopious Catholic Church

Saint Anthony's Catholic Church, Pukwana, 1909 [6/18/2010]

Saint Olaf Lutheran Church, Ola, 1910 [6/18/2010]

Pukwana Lutheran Church, Pukwana, 1928 [6/26/2009]

Dunlap Methodist Episcopal Church, 12 miles north of Platte, 1906 [5/22/2012]

Saint Margaret's Catholic Church, Kimball, 1916 [6/19/2005]

Unknown church, Bijou Hills, date unknown [6/19/2005]

BUFFALO COUNTY

Saint Peter's Episcopal Church, rural Buffalo County, 1895 (rebuilt after storm in 1924) [5/25/2006]

Unknown church, rural Buffalo County, date unknown [5/22/2006]

Saint Placidus Duncan Catholic Church, 10 miles north, 3.5 miles west of Gann Valley, 1899 (rebuilt after storms in 1925 and 1927) [7/17/2009]

Saint John's Episcopal Church, 3 miles west of Shelby, date unknown [6/18/2010]

BUTTE COUNTY

Saint James Episcopal Church, Belle Fourche, 1909
[8/4/2006]

First Congregational Church, Newell, 1912
(originally Methodist) [7/27/2007]

Newell Christian Fellowship, Newell, 1912
(Methodist Episcopal until 1937) [7/27/2007]

CAMPBELL COUNTY

Norway Lutheran Church, 4 miles south, 5 miles west of
Mound City, 1897 [5/26/2010]

Church of God, Mound City, 1898 (Methodist until 1942)
[5/26/2010]

Artas Baptist Church, Artas, 1906, closed 1964, repurposed as city hall but no longer used [5/19/2008]

Artas Reformed Church, Artas, 1907, closed 1997, repurposed as a home [5/19/2008]

Grace Congregational Church, Mobridge, 1910 (Catholic church until 1948) [5/25/2012]

First Baptist Church, Mobridge, 1929 [5/19/2008]

CHARLES MIX COUNTY

Old Cedar Presbyterian Church, Pickstown, ca. 1877 [6/16/2010]

Academy Congregational Church, Academy, 1898 [7/7/2008]

First Lutheran Church, Lake Andes, 1909, remodeled 1945 [7/7/2008]

Saint John's Catholic Church, Wagner, 1911 [6/7/2006]

East Lake Andes Lutheran Church, 9 miles south of Armour, 1913 (Saint Theresa Catholic in Delmont until 1967) [7/7/2008]

Saint John the Evangelist Catholic Mission, Greenwood, 1914 [6/24/2006]

West Trinity Church, 10 miles west, 1 mile south of Platte, 1914, closed 1970 [7/7/2008]

Saint Paul's Lutheran Church, 7 miles south of Delmont, 1914 [6/16/2010]

Saint Peter's Episcopal Church, Lake Andes, 1917 [5/22/2012]

United Methodist Church, Geddes, 1925 (originally Community Methodist Episcopal Church) [7/7/2008]

Ihanktonwan Owakpamni Presbyterian Church, Greenwood, 1917 [6/24/2006]

First Presbyterian Church, Lake Andes, 1918 [7/7/2008]

Cedar Presbyterian Church, Pickstown, date unknown [6/16/2010]

Grace Baptist Church, Lake Andes, date unknown [7/7/2008]

CLARK COUNTY

Good Hope Lutheran Church, 8 miles north of Vienna, 1890 [8/13/2007]

United Methodist Church, 2 miles east, 1 mile south of Carpenter, 1893 [8/13/2007]

Telemarken Lutheran Church, 2 miles west, 3 miles north of Wallace, 1894 [5/27/2010]

Clark Center Lutheran Church, 3 miles west, 5 miles north of Clark, 1898 [8/13/2007]

Saint James Catholic Church, Willow Lake, 1905 [8/13/2007]

United Church of Christ, Willow Lake, 1905 [5/27/2010]

Naples Lutheran Church, Naples, 1906 [7/20/2007]

Bethlehem Evangelical Lutheran Church, Raymond, 1907 [8/13/2007]

Bethlehem Lutheran Church, Vienna, 1910 [8/13/2007]

Crandall Community Church, Clark, 1911 [8/13/2007]

Calvary Lutheran Church, 3 miles west, 2 miles south of Bradley, 1914 [8/13/2007]

Interior, Calvary Lutheran Church

Crocker Lutheran Church, Crocker, date unknown (originally a bank until 1918) [8/13/2007]

First Presbyterian Church, Raymond, 1920 [8/13/2007]

Presbyterian Church United, Willow Lake, 1921 [8/13/2007]

Unknown church, Garden City, date unknown [8/13/2007]

CLAY COUNTY

Westreville Pleasant Valley Lutheran Church, 9 miles north, 3 miles west of Vermillion, 1885 [7/14/2009]

United Church of Christ, Wakonda, 1886 [6/8/2006]

Dalesburg Lutheran Church, Hub City, 1896 (back section), 1920 (middle), 1984 (front) [6/8/2006]

First Baptist Church, Vermillion, 1899 [5/24/2006]

Komstad Covenant Church, 6 miles north of Hub City, 1906 [6/8/2006]

Saint Patrick's Catholic Church, Wakonda, 1904 [6/8/2006]

Volin Lutheran Church, Volin, 1908 [7/14/2009]

Bergen Lutheran Church, 6 miles south of Meckling, 1911 [6/19/2006]

United Methodist Church, Wakonda, 1914 [6/8/2006]

Bethel Baptist Church, Wakonda, 1914 [6/7/2006]

Dalesburg Baptist Church, 1 mile east, 1 mile north of Hub City, 1919 (originally Bloomingdale Swedish Baptist Church) [6/8/2006]

United Church of Christ Congregational, Vermillion, 1928 [6/7/2006]

First Methodist Episcopal Church, Vermillion, 1929 [6/8/2006]

CODINGTON COUNTY

United Methodist Church, Henry, 1882 [5/20/2009]

New Helgen Lutheran Church, Florence, 1889 [5/20/2009]

Saint John Evangelical Lutheran Church, 9 miles north, 1 mile east of Watertown, 1890 [7/20/2007]

Graceland Church, 6 miles north of Henry, 1892, closed 1945 [5/20/2009]

Holy Rosary Catholic Church, Kranzburg, 1898 [9/9/2013]

Saint Peter's Catholic Church, Grover, 1901 [7/20/2007]

Saint Pauli Lutheran Church, 4 miles north of Wallace, 1901 [5/20/2009]

Goodhue Lutheran Church, 4 miles north, 3 miles west of Florence, 1904, addition 1947 [5/20/2009]

Saint Henry's Catholic Church, Henry, 1907 [5/20/2009]

Florence Methodist Church, Florence, 1908 [5/20/2009]

First United Methodist Church, Watertown, 1915 [7/20/2007]

First Congregational Church, Watertown, 1916 [7/20/2007]

Saint Paul's Lutheran Church, Henry, 1918 [5/20/2009]

Blessed Sacrament Catholic Church, Florence, 1919 [5/20/2009]

Grace Lutheran Church, Watertown, 1920 [7/20/2007]

CORSON COUNTY

Chapel of the Holy Spirit (Episcopal), 7 miles north, 2 miles west of Firesteel, 1923 [8/18/2005]

First Presbyterian Church, McIntosh, 1924 [8/19/2005]

Saint Paul's Lutheran Church, McIntosh, 1924 [6/19/2010]

Christ Lutheran Church, Morristown, 1926 [7/28/2007]

Saint Michael's Catholic Church, Watauga, 1928 [7/28/2007]

Saint Bede Catholic Church, Wakpala, 1928 [5/25/2010]

Saint Elizabeth's Episcopal Church, Wakpala, 1929 [5/26/2010]

Church of God, McIntosh, date unknown [8/19/2005]

Unknown church, Morristown, date unknown [7/28/2007]

Saint John's Catholic Church, Watauga, date unknown [7/28/2007]

CUSTER COUNTY

United Church of Christ, Hermosa, 1889, addition 1924 (President Calvin Coolidge attended services here in 1927) [7/8/2007]

Buffalo Gap United Methodist Church, Buffalo Gap, 1889 [6/20/2010]

Pringle Methodist Church, Pringle, 1898 [9/7/2013]

Saint Michael's Catholic Church, Hermosa, 1922 [7/8/2007]

DAVISON COUNTY

United Methodist Church, Mount Vernon, 1883 [7/10/2008]

First United Methodist Church, Mitchell, 1907 [7/17/2009]

Congregational United Church of Christ, Mitchell, 1908 [7/10/2008]

Holy Family Catholic Church, Mitchell, 1908 [6/17/2010]

Farwell United Methodist Church, Mitchell, 1908, now part of a museum [9/17/2009]

Saint Mary's Episcopal Church, Mitchell, 1912 [7/10/2008]

Immanuel Lutheran Church, 3 miles north, 1 mile west of Mount Vernon, 1923 [7/10/2008]

DAY COUNTY

Butler Lutheran Church, Butler, 1886 [5/20/2009]

United Methodist Church, Andover, 1886, closed 2002 [5/21/2009]

North Highland United Methodist Church, Andover, 1886 [5/21/2009]

Pierpont Community Church, Pierpont, 1889 (originally First Baptist) [5/21/2009]

Bristol-Butler United Methodist Church, Bristol, 1889 (originally First Methodist Episcopal Church) [5/25/2012]

Skudesnes Evangelical Lutheran Church, 8 miles east, 0.5 miles south of Pierpont, 1891 [5/21/2009]

First Nation Church, Waubay, 1897 (originally United Church of Christ) [7/18/2007]

Saint Mary's Episcopal Church, Webster, 1900 [7/19/2007]

Tabor Lutheran Church, 7 miles north, 3 miles west of Webster, 1902 [5/21/2009]

Buffalo Plains Historical Church, Lily, 1903 (originally Lily Lutheran) [5/20/2009]

Our Savior Lutheran Church, Waubay, 1913 (originally Norwegian Lutheran) [7/18/2007]

American Lutheran Church, Webster, 1916 [7/19/2007]

Zion Evangelical Lutheran Church, Waubay, 1925 [5/27/2010]

Egeland Lutheran Church, 9 miles north, 1 mile west of Florence, 1926 [5/20/2009]

All Saints Catholic Church, Andover, date unknown (moved from Mina in Brown County in 1938) [5/21/2009]

DEUEL COUNTY

Bemis Holland Presbyterian Church, 4 miles south, 1 mile west of Bemis, 1882 [8/18/2008]

United Methodist Church, Gary, 1883 [7/16/2009]

Blom Prairie Lutheran Brethren Church, Toronto, 1892 [8/18/2008]

Highland Lutheran Church, Brandt, 1892 [8/18/2008]

Saint Peter's Evangelical Lutheran Church, Goodwin, 1898 [5/22/2009]

Zoar Lutheran Church, 4 miles south, 5.5 miles east of Revillo, 1901, addition 1949 [7/16/2007]

Congregational Church, Clear Lake, 1903 [8/18/2008]

Antelope Valley Reformed Church, 6 miles south, 3.5 miles east of Revillo, 1907 (originally Methodist church in Mehurin Township, moved in 1922) [7/16/2007]

East Highland Lutheran Church, 1 mile north, 5 miles east of Brandt, 1916 [8/18/2008]

Wood Lake Lutheran Church, 4 miles north, 2 miles east of Astoria, 1924 [8/18/2008]

DEWEY COUNTY

Emmanuel Episcopal Church, 1.5 miles east of White Horse, 1887 [6/19/2010]

Saint Thomas Episcopal Station, On the Tree, 7 miles east of Highway 63 on BIA2, 1889 [6/19/2010]

Saint Joseph's Catholic Church, Ridgeview, 1892 (originally Corpus Christi, moved in 1959 because of Oahe Dam) [8/17/2007]

United Church of Christ, La Plant, 1910 [8/18/2007]

La Plant Baptist Church, La Plant, 1910 (formerly a Catholic church) [5/26/2012]

Church of God of Prophecy, Isabel, 1916, now a business [6/19/2010]

Saint Basil's Catholic Church, Mossman, 1917 [6/19/2010]

Protestant Reformed Church, Isabel, 1918 [6/19/2010]

Unknown Lutheran church, Trail City, 1919 [8/19/2005]

Saint Mary's Catholic Church, Isabel, 1920 [6/19/2010]

Our Savior's Lutheran Church, 3 miles north, 1 mile east of Firesteel, 1927, closed 1964 [8/19/2005]

Emmanuel Lutheran Church, Eagle Butte, date unknown [8/17/2007]

DOUGLAS COUNTY

First Reformed Church, Harrison, 1883, addition 1920 [7/8/2008]

Christian Reformed Church, Harrison, 1884 [7/8/2008]

Bethany United Church of Christ, Delmont, 1894, now a hunting lodge [5/22/2012]

Grandview Reformed Church, Armour, 1902 (built as Saint John's Lutheran in Hillside) [7/7/2008]

Zion Lutheran Church, Delmont, 1912 [5/22/2012]

Immanuel Lutheran Church, 8 miles west of Dimock, 1914 [6/23/2006]

Christian Reformed Church, New Holland, 1920 [7/8/2008]

Interior, Christian Reformed Church

Saint Peter's Lutheran Church, 4 miles north, 5 miles east of Armour, 1924 [6/16/2010]

Interior, Saint Peter's Lutheran Church

Hope Lutheran Church, Delmont, 1928 [5/22/2012]

EDMUNDS COUNTY

Congregational United Church of Christ, Ipswich, 1884 [8/16/2007]

Powell Presbyterian Church, Ipswich, 1886 [5/26/2010]

Roscoe Presbyterian Church, Roscoe, 1886, closed 2007 [8/16/2007]

Evangel United Methodist Church, Bowdle, 1887 (Congregational church 1887–1958), closed 1979 [8/16/2007]

Bowdle Methodist Church, Bowdle, 1895, sold to Gospel Tabernacle in 1969, now apartments [8/16/2007]

Saint Augustine's Catholic Church, Bowdle, 1918 [8/16/2007]

Hosmer Reformed Church, Hosmer, 1925 [8/16/2007]

First Baptist Church, Ipswich, 1926 [8/16/2007]

Saint Paul's Evangelical Lutheran Church, Roscoe, 1928 [7/17/2009]

FALL RIVER COUNTY

United Methodist Church, Oelrichs, 1888 [6/24/2009]

Saint Luke's Episcopal Church, Hot Springs, 1902 [7/5/2007]

Bethesda Evangelical Lutheran Church, Hot Springs, 1923, now a photo studio [6/20/2010]

First Congregational Church, Edgemont, 1926 [7/5/2007]

Saint Martin's Catholic Church, Oelrichs, date unknown, closed 1999 [6/20/2010]

FAULK COUNTY

DeVoe Methodist Church, Cresbard, 1887 (moved from Myron Township), now a museum [7/5/2007]

Old Congregational Church, Cresbard, 1890 [5/25/2012]

United Methodist Church, Rockham, 1908 [8/17/2007]

Miranda Methodist Church, Miranda, 1909, closed 2005 [5/25/2012]

Saint Joseph's Catholic Church, Orient, 1910 [6/18/2010]

Sacred Heart Catholic Church, Chelsea, 1910, closed 2005 [8/17/2007]

Norbeck Baptist Church, Norbeck, 1913 (moved from Orleans) [8/17/2007]

Orient Lutheran Church, Orient, 1919 [8/17/2007]

First Lutheran Church, Faulkton, 1922 (formerly Trinity Lutheran, near Bowdle, moved in 1947) [7/17/2009]

Zion Lutheran Church, Rockham, 1925, closed 1974 [8/17/2007]

United Methodist Church, Seneca, 1926 [8/17/2007]

GRANT COUNTY

Brown Earth Presbyterian Church, 2 miles north, 2 miles east of Stockholm, 1877 [7/16/2007]

Saint Charles Borromeo Catholic Church, Big Stone City, 1882 [5/22/2009]

Congregational United Church of Christ, Milbank, 1883 [7/16/2007]

Bethlehem Lutheran Church, 5 miles east of Milbank, 1892 [7/16/2007]

Christ Episcopal Church, Milbank, 1903 [5/24/2012]

Trinity Lutheran Church, Revillo, 1890, narthex added 1981 [5/23/2012]

Evangelical Covenant Church, LaBolt, 1900 [7/16/2007]

Valley Baptist Church, Milbank, 1907 (Emmanuel Evangelical Lutheran until 1957) [7/17/2007]

Lebanon Lutheran Church, 2 miles south, 3 miles west of Summit, 1908 [7/17/2007]

Marvin Baptist Church, Marvin, 1908 [7/16/2007]

Tabor Lutheran Church, Strandburg, 1910 [7/16/2007]

Saint Lawrence Catholic Church, Milbank, 1913 [5/27/2010]

Martin Evangelical Lutheran Church, Marvin, 1919 (formerly Bethel Lutheran) [7/16/2007]

Elim Evangelical Covenant Church, Stockholm, date unknown (moved from Bemis in 1948) [5/24/2012]

Zion Presbyterian Church, Twin Brooks, date unknown (Methodist until about 1965) [7/16/2007]

GREGORY COUNTY

Trinity Lutheran Church, Fairfax, 1904 (originally Methodist) [6/15/2010]

Saint John Evangelist Catholic Church, Herrick, 1908 [6/6/2006]

Union Baptist Church, Burke, 1908 [5/22/2012]

First Baptist Church, Lucas, 1908 [5/21/2012]

Saint John's Catholic Church, Paxton, 1915, on the National Register of Historic Places, closed 1973 [6/6/2006]

Peace Lutheran Church, Carlock, 1920 [6/6/2006]

Saint Augustine's Catholic Church, Dallas, 1924, now owned by Gregory County Historical Society [6/6/2006]

Unknown Methodist church, Dallas, date unknown [6/6/2006]

Hope Congregational Church of Christ, Fairfax, date unknown [6/15/2010]

HAAKON COUNTY

Deep Creek Lutheran Church, 11 miles north, 13 miles west of Hayes, 1924 (built in Kirley) [9/4/2005]

HAMLIN COUNTY

Hazel United Methodist Church, Hazel, 1891 [7/20/2007]

New Hope Lutheran Church, 4.5 miles east, 3 miles south of Hazel, 1891 [7/20/2007]

First Evangelical Lutheran Church, Lake Norden, 1891, now Lake Norden Historical Society Museum [8/16/2008]

United Church of Christ, Bryant, 1896 [7/16/2009]

Kellerton United Methodist Church, 1.5 miles east, 2 miles south of Hazel, 1898 [7/20/2007]

United Church of Christ, Estelline, 1903 [8/16/2008]

Apostolic Lutheran Church, Lake Norden, 1908 (National Lutheran until 1947) [8/16/2008]

Garfield Lutheran Church, 6 miles east of Bryant, 1902 [8/16/2008]

Lake Norden Baptist Church, Lake Norden, 1909 [7/16/2009]

Trinity Lutheran Church, Lake Norden, 1909 (formerly Emmanuel Lutheran) [8/15/2008]

First Presbyterian Church, Castlewood, 1915 [8/16/2008]

Our Savior Lutheran Church, 3 miles north, 3.5 miles west of Hazel, 1926 [5/27/2010]

Saint John's Lutheran Church, Dempster, 1913 (originally a school, steeple added in 1944) [8/16/2008]

HAND COUNTY

Ree Heights Community Church, Ree Heights, 1885 [5/21/2008]

Saint Lawrence Community Church, Saint Lawrence, 1885 (originally Methodist or Presbyterian) [5/21/2008]

Beulah Community Church, 8 miles north of former site of Vayland, 1886 [5/21/2008]

Pleasant Valley Church, 17 miles south of Miller, 1894 [7/17/2009]

Saint Mary's Catholic Church, Zell, 1906 [6/18/2010]

Rose Hill Presbyterian Church, 13 miles south of former site of Vayland, 1918 [5/21/2008]

Saint Liborius Catholic Church, Polo, 1920 [5/25/2012]

Greenleaf United Methodist Church, 7 miles north, 4 miles west of Miller, 1926 [5/21/2008]

First Presbyterian Church, Miller, 1929 [5/21/2008]

HANSON COUNTY

Saint Martin's Lutheran Church, Alexandria, 1885 [7/17/2009]

Church of the Epiphany (Catholic), Epiphany, 1901 [5/23/2012]

Saint Mary of Mercy Catholic Church, Alexandria, 1907 [8/7/2006]

Saint Paul's Presbyterian Church, Emery, 1923 [8/7/2006]

Fulton Christian Fellowship Church, Fulton, 1920 (originally Methodist-Episcopalian) [6/8/2007]

Saint John's Lutheran Church, Emery, 1927 [8/7/2006]

Unknown Presbyterian church, Emery, unknown [6/17/2010]

HARDING COUNTY

United Methodist Church, Camp Crook, 1909 [7/29/2007]

Ralph Lutheran Church, Ralph, 1913 [6/24/2009]

Our Lady of the Prairie, Reva, 1917 (front section built as Saint Eulalia's Church in Ralph; rear section built as Sacred Heart Church in Strool, Perkins County), buildings consolidated in 1957 [8/4/2005]

Saint Ann's Catholic Church, Camp Crook, 1910 [7/29/2007]

Buffalo Congregational Church, Buffalo, 1914 [6/24/2009]

Peace Evangelical United Brethren Church, 4 miles east, 5 miles north of Ralph, 1919 [6/24/2009]

Golden Valley Norwegian Lutheran Church, 5.5 miles east, 7.5 miles north of Ralph, 1921 [9/11/2010]

Interior, Golden Valley Norwegian Lutheran Church

Saint Agnes Catholic Church, 6 miles north, 5 miles west of Ludlow, 1926 [6/24/2009]

Saint Agnes Catholic Church from a distance

Slim Buttes Lutheran Church, 2.5 miles east of Reva, 1928 [6/24/2009]

Cave Hills Lutheran Church, 6 miles north of Buffalo, 1929 [9/11/2010]

Ladner Lutheran Church, Ladner, date unknown [9/11/2010]

HUGHES COUNTY

Oahe Chapel, 5 miles north, 1 mile west of Pierre, 1877 [5/25/2010]

United Methodist Church, Pierre, 1910 [5/21/2008]

Immanuel Lutheran Church, Harrold, 1925 [5/21/2008]

Unknown Catholic church, Blunt, date unknown [5/21/2008]

HUTCHINSON COUNTY

Johannesthal Reformed Church, Freeman, 1902, now part of museum [6/23/2006]

Interior, Johannesthal Reformed Church

Saints Peter and Paul Catholic Church, Dimock, 1908 [6/23/2006]

Interior, Saints Peter and Paul Catholic Church

First American Lutheran Church, Tripp, 1910 (originally First Evangelical Lutheran) [6/23/2006]

Emmaus Lutheran Church, Tripp, 1913 [5/22/2012]

Bethel Mennonite Church, Freeman, 1920 (moved from original location north of Freeman in 1992), part of museum [6/23/2006]

Salem Lutheran Church, Parkston, 1926 [5/22/2012]

Unity Lutheran Church, Menno, 1929 (built near Clayton), now part of Pioneer Acres Museum [8/7/2006]

Baptist church, Tripp, date unknown [5/22/2012]

HYDE COUNTY

United Methodist Church, Highmore, 1886, brick veneer added in 1965 [5/21/2008]

Grace Bible Church, Highmore, 1889 [5/21/2008]

Church of Christ, Highmore, 1904 [5/21/2008]

Our Savior Lutheran Church, 16 miles north, 4 miles west of Highmore, 1909 [5/21/2008]

Saint Mary's Catholic Church, Highmore, 1922, now Saint Theresa's Hall [5/21/2008]

JACKSON COUNTY

Congregational church, Cottonwood, 1908 [9/4/2005]

First Presbyterian Church, Belvidere, 1909 [6/19/2010]

Gethsemane Episcopal Church, Wanblee, 1910 [6/15/2010]

Church of Saint Henry (Catholic), Potato Creek, 1911 [9/9/2010]

Church of the Holy Rosary (Catholic), Interior, 1911 [9/9/2010]

First Presbyterian Church, Interior, 1911 [9/9/2010]

Saint Stephen's Catholic Church, northeast of Belvidere at 1880 Town, 1915 (built in Dixon, Gregory County) [6/18/2010]

Unknown church, Wanblee, date unknown [9/4/2005]

Big Foot Pass Presbyterian Church, northeast of Belvidere at 1880 Town, date unknown [6/18/2010]

JERAULD COUNTY

United Church of Christ, Wessington Springs, 1898 [6/17/2010]

Zion Emmanuel Lutheran Church, Lane, 1910, Lane Community Center since 1965 [7/9/2008]

United Methodist Church, Lane, 1910 [7/9/2008]

United Methodist Church, Wessington Springs, 1913 [7/8/2008]

Harmony Friends Church, 9 miles west, 3 miles north of Wessington Springs, 1913 [7/8/2008]

Zion Lutheran Church, Wessington Springs, 1916 [7/17/2009]

Templeton United Church of Christ, 7 miles west, 1 mile south of Wessington Springs, 1925 [7/8/2008]

JONES COUNTY

Saint Anthony's Catholic Church, Draper, 1911 [6/26/2009]

KINGSBURY COUNTY

Christian and Missionary Alliance Church, De Smet, 1882 (First Congregational until 1969) [5/20/2009]

United Methodist Church, De Smet, 1885 [5/20/2009]

Esmond United Methodist Church, Esmond, 1885 [5/20/2009]

Erwin United Church of Christ, Erwin, 1888, enlarged in 1913 [5/20/2009]

Orthodox Presbyterian Church, Bancroft, 1889 [5/20/2009]

Spring Lake Covenant, 6 miles south, 5 miles west of Arlington, 1891 [5/19/2009]

Lake Whitewood Lutheran Church, 3 miles south, 5 miles west of Arlington, 1893 [5/19/2009]

Trinity Lutheran Church, 3 miles west of Oldham, 1898 [5/28/2010]

Hetland Congregational Church, Hetland, 1899 [5/19/2009]

West Bethany Lutheran Church, 1 mile south, 1 mile east of De Smet, 1905 [5/19/2009]

Saint John's Lutheran Church, Bancroft, 1908 [5/20/2009]

United Methodist Church, Lake Preston, 1908 [5/19/2009]

Spirit Lake Presbyterian Church, 9 miles west, 2 miles north of Erwin, 1908 [5/20/2009]

United Church of Christ, Lake Preston, 1910 [5/19/2009]

Saint Stephen Episcopal Church, De Smet, 1910 [5/20/2009]

United Methodist Church, Arlington, 1919 [5/19/2009]

First Evangelical Lutheran Church, Badger, 1925 [5/20/2009]

Saint Thomas Aquinas Catholic Church, De Smet, 1929 [5/20/2009]

North Preston Lutheran Church, 6 miles east, 3 miles south of Erwin, 1929 [5/20/2009]

LAKE COUNTY

First Baptist Church, Madison, 1881 [8/7/2006]

Saint Ann's Catholic Church, 2 miles north, 2.5 miles east of Ramona, 1884 [5/28/2010]

First Baptist Church, Madison, 1889 (second church in Madison to use this name) [8/8/2006]

First Presbyterian Church, Madison, 1892 [5/23/2012]

Grace Episcopal Church, Madison, 1893 [8/8/2006]

Lake Madison Lutheran Church, 5 miles south, 1.5 miles west of Nunda, 1898 [8/8/2006]

Saint William's Catholic Church, Ramona, 1899 [8/9/2006]

Interior, Saint William's Catholic Church

Prairie Village Church, west of Madison, 1906 [8/7/2006]

United Methodist Church, Madison, 1906 [5/23/2012]

First Presbyterian Church, Wentworth, 1914 [8/8/2006]

Seventh Day Adventist Church, Madison, 1907 [8/7/2006]

Saint Thomas Aquinas Catholic Church, Madison, 1918 [8/8/2006]

Interior, Saint Thomas Aquinas Catholic Church

United Methodist Church, Chester, 1918 [8/8/2006]

United Church of Christ, Winfred, 1919 [7/17/2009]

Trinity Lutheran Church, Madison, 1920 [5/23/2012]

West Center Baptist Church, Madison, 1921 [8/8/2006]

LAWRENCE COUNTY

Saint Lawrence O'Toole Catholic Church, Central City, 1878 [7/30/2007]

Saint John's Episcopal Church, Deadwood, 1881 [9/11/2010]

First Presbyterian Church, Whitewood, 1888 [7/29/2007]

Finnish Evangelical Lutheran Church, Lead, 1889, now a business [7/30/2007]

All Angels Episcopal Church, Spearfish, 1895 [7/7/2007]

Christ Church (Episcopal), Lead, 1896 [7/30/2007]

First Baptist Church, Deadwood, 1917 [7/30/2007]

LINCOLN COUNTY

Saint Edward's Catholic Church, Worthing, 1888 [7/15/2009]

First Congregational Church, Hudson, 1891 [7/15/2009]

United Church of Christ Congregational, Beresford, 1893 [6/8/2006]

Worthing Community Church, Worthing, 1900 [7/15/2009]

Romsdal Lutheran Church, 3 miles west of site of Moe, 1903 [6/17/2010]

Saint Nicholas Catholic Church, Tea, 1906, now a museum [7/15/2009]

Trinity Lutheran Church, at site of Moe, 1904 [6/19/2006]

Springdale Lutheran Church, 4 miles east, 4 miles north of Harrisburg, 1907 [7/15/2006]

Grand Valley Lutheran Church, 2 miles west, 3 miles south of Canton, 1909 [6/28/2009]

Canton Lutheran Church, Canton, 1910 [6/19/2006]

Rearview, Canton Lutheran

Interior, Canton Lutheran

Skrefsrud Lutheran Church, 5 miles north, 1 mile west of Beresford, 1911 [6/19/2006]

Ebenezer Presbyterian Church, Lennox, 1917 [6/19/2006]

Brooklyn Evangelical Free Church, 3 miles west of Beresford, 1918 [6/19/2006]

LYMAN COUNTY

Saint Augustine Catholic Church, Presho, 1904 (built in Sweeney), now part of Presho Museum [6/18/2010]

United Methodist Church, Kennebec, 1907 [6/26/2009]

Vivian Methodist Church, Vivian, 1907 [8/5/2005]

Sacred Heart Catholic Church, Vivian, 1915 (built as Saint Mary's Catholic in Okaton, moved 1953) [8/5/2005]

McCOOK COUNTY

Evangelical Covenant Church, 6 miles north of Salem, 1885 [6/22/2006]

Salem Evangelical Lutheran Church, 7 miles north, 2 miles east of Salem, 1891 [6/22/2006]

Saint Mary's Catholic Church, Salem, 1898 [6/22/2006]

Interior, Saint Mary's Catholic Church

Saint Patrick's Catholic Church, Montrose, 1906 [6/21/2006]

Interior, Saint Patrick's Catholic Church

Immanuel Lutheran Church, 8 miles north, 6 miles west of Salem, 1914 [6/22/2006]

Altar, Immanuel Lutheran Church

Christ Lutheran Church, Salem, 1915 [6/22/2006]

Ramsey Baptist Church, 8 miles north, 8 miles east of Salem, 1918 [6/22/2006]

Sun Prairie Baptist Church, 9 miles north, 1 mile west of Salem, 1918 [6/22/2006]

Trinity Orthodox Presbyterian Church, Bridgewater, 1928 [6/22/2006]

United Methodist Church, Leola, 1889 [8/16/2007]

Our Lady of Perpetual Help Catholic Church, Leola, 1916 [8/16/2007]

Saint Paul's Lutheran Church, Leola, 1922 [5/25/2012]

Seventh Day Adventist Church, Leola, 1925 [8/16/2007]

Zion Lutheran Church, Eureka, 1926 [8/16/2007]

MARSHALL COUNTY

Highlanda Lutheran Church, 6 miles east, 1 mile north of Langford, 1893 [10/9/2010]

Buffalo Lake Presbyterian Church, 4.5 miles east, .05 mile south of Eden, 1901 [7/10/2007]

Palestine Lutheran Church, 4 miles north, 2 miles east of Veblen, 1903 [7/18/2007]

Lake City Lutheran Church, Lake City, 1893 (built in Britton, moved 1950) [5/24/2012]

Veblen Presbyterian Church, Veblen, 1903 [7/18/2007]

Buffalo Lake Lutheran Church, 2 miles north, 9 miles west of Peever, 1904 [7/17/2007]

Saint John Nepomucene Catholic Church, Veblen, 1907 [7/18/2007]

Pleasant Valley Lutheran Church, 7 miles north, 4 miles east of Britton, 1908 [5/25/2012]

Saint John's Lutheran Church, Britton, 1917 [5/26/2010]

Saint John de Britto Catholic Church, Britton, 1917 [9/10/2010]

Zion Lutheran Church, 4 miles south, 4 miles west of Veblen, 1919 [9/10/2010]

Interior, Zion Lutheran Church

Zion Reformed Church, Amherst, 1921 [7/18/2007]

First Presbyterian Church, Britton, 1922 [7/18/2007]

United Methodist Church, Langford, 1923 [7/18/2007]

MEADE COUNTY

Christian Family Assembly of God Church, Sturgis, 1887 (originally Methodist Episcopal) [7/27/2007]

Saint Thomas Episcopal Church, Sturgis, 1892 [7/27/2007]

Saint Martin's Chapel (Catholic), Sturgis, 1911 [7/27/2007]

First Congregational Church, Sturgis, 1911 [7/27/007]

Saint Paul's Evangelical Lutheran Church, Faith, 1914 [7/27/2007]

Faith Christian Center, Faith, 1917 (originally Saint Joseph's Catholic Church) [5/26/2012]

Our Lady of Victory Catholic Church, Plainview, 1918 (town gone) [7/28/2007]

Marcus Presbyterian Church, Marcus, 1921 [5/26/2012]

Saint Anthony's Catholic Church, Red Owl, 1921 [5/26/2012]

Saint Joseph's Catholic Church, Mud Butte, 1921 [5/26/2012]

Bethel Lutheran Church, Faith, 1925 [5/26/2012]

Saint Ignatius Catholic Church, White River, 1899
[5/29/2010]

Our Lady of Good Council Catholic Church, Wood, 1910
[6/15/2010]

Interior, Our Lady of Good Council Catholic Church

Happy Hollow Congregational Church, Wood, 1916
[8/17/2005]

United Methodist Church, White River, 1919
[5/29/2010]

Sacred Heart Catholic Church, White River, 1920 [5/29/2010]

Saint Paul's Evangelical Lutheran Church, White River, 1927 [9/3/2005]

Holy Family Catholic Church, 7 miles north, 3 miles west of Mission, 1927 [5/21/2012]

Interior, Holy Family Catholic Church

Saint Peter's Catholic Church, Wood, date unknown (moved to Wood in 1933) [8/17/2005]

Zion Lutheran Church, Wood, date unknown [8/17/2005]

Church of the Sacred Heart (Catholic), Norris, date unknown (moved from Red Leaf in 1955) [6/15/2010]

MINER COUNTY

German Methodist Church, Howard, 1882 [8/7/2006]

Congregational United Church of Christ, Canova, 1889 [6/22/2006]

United Church of Christ Congregational, Carthage, 1890 (built in Esmond, moved ca. 1894–1895) [8/10/2006]

Trinity Lutheran Church, Carthage, 1899 (formerly Zion Lutheran) [5/28/2010]

Church of Christ, Carthage, 1906, closed 1960s, now a woodworking shop [8/10/2006]

Endeavor Presbyterian Church, Fedora, 1911 [8/7/2006]

Saint John's Lutheran Church, Howard, 1911 [8/7/2006]

Union Presbyterian Church, 3 miles north, 4.5 miles east of Canova, 1915 [5/23/2012]

Belleview Lutheran Church, 7 miles north, 2 miles east of Howard, 1916 [8/10/2006]

Roswell Methodist Church, Roswell, date unknown [8/7/2006]

Grace Bible Church, Valley Springs, 1878 (originally United Church of Christ) [6/20/2006]

Valley Springs Reformed Church, Valley Springs, 1884 (formerly Congregational) [6/20/2006]

Renner Lutheran Church, Renner, 1878 (originally Nidaros Lutheran southeast of town) [6/21/2006]

First Baptist Church, Dell Rapids, 1884 [5/28/2010]

Church of the Good Samaritan, Sioux Falls, ca. 1890 (moved from Parker to Sioux Empire Fairgrounds) [5/23/2012]

Beaver Creek Lutheran Church, Sioux Falls, 1892, on Augustana University campus [5/28/2010]

Willow Creek Lutheran Church, 4 miles east of Colton, 1893 [6/21/2006]

Church of the Living Waters (Episcopal), Dell Rapids, 1893, now used as a home [6/21/2006]

United Methodist Church, Ben Clare, 1894 [6/28/2009]

Saint Jacob's Lutheran Church, 1 mile north, 5 miles west of Colton, 1897 [9/10/2010]

Baltic Lutheran Church, Baltic, 1903 [5/28/2010]

First Lutheran Church, Sherman, 1899 [5/28/2010]

Dell Rapids Lutheran Church, Dell Rapids, 1902 [6/21/2006]

Rowena United Methodist Church, Rowena, 1903 [5/23/2012]

Trinity Lutheran Church, 1 mile north of Ellis, 1905 [7/15/2009]

Faith Family Church, Sioux Falls, 1908 [6/20/2006]

United Methodist Church, Colton, 1906 (formerly Methodist Episcopal) [6/21/2006]

Saint Rose of Lima Catholic Church, Garretson, 1907 [6/26/2009]

First Congregational United Church of Christ, Sioux Falls, 1909 [6/20/2006]

East Nidaros Lutheran Church, 2 miles south, 2 miles west of Baltic, 1911 [6/21/2006]

West Nidaros Lutheran Church, 3 miles south, 3 miles west of Baltic, 1911 [6/21/2006]

Interior, West Nidaros Lutheran Church

First United Methodist Church, Sioux Falls, 1913 (formerly Methodist Episcopal) [6/20/2006]

Benton Lutheran Church, 2 miles west of Crooks, 1915 [6/21/2006]

First Lutheran Church, Colton, 1918 [7/15/2009]

Cathedral of Saint Joseph, Sioux Falls, 1919 [6/20/2006]

Saint George's Catholic Church, Hartford, 1920 [9/10/2010]

Beaver Valley Lutheran Church, Valley Springs, 1922 [5/28/2006]

First Christian Church, Sioux Falls, 1925 [5/28/2010]

First Lutheran Church, Sioux Falls, 1925 [6/20/2006]

Highland Lutheran Church, 4 miles north, 2 miles west of Sherman, 1922 [5/28/2010]

Our Lady of Guadalupe Catholic Church, Sioux Falls, 1925 (formerly Little Flower of Jesus) [6/20/2006]

Split Rock Lutheran Church, 3 miles north, 1 mile east of Brandon, date unknown [5/28/2010]

MOODY COUNTYVAV

First Presbyterian Church, Flandreau, 1873 [8/9/2006]

Redeemer Lutheran Church, Egan, 1880 (originally Methodist, then a school 1912–1922, Redeemer Lutheran until 1961, American Legion Hall, 1962–2006) [8/9/2006]

Immanuel Evangelical Lutheran Church, Ward, 1902 [8/9/2006]

Sioux Valley Baptist Church, 2.5 miles south of Trent, 1888 [8/8/2006]

Lone Rock Lutheran Church, 2 miles south, 8 miles east of Egan, 1903 [8/8/2006]

West Baptist Memorial Chapel, 4 miles east of Chester, 1909 [8/8/2006]

United Methodist Church, Colman, 1905 [8/8/2006]

Second Presbyterian Church, Flandreau, 1905 [8/8/2006]

United Methodist Church, Egan, 1911 (originally Methodist Episcopal) [8/9/2006]

Trent Baptist Church, Trent, 1912 [8/8/2006]

Saints Simon and Jude Catholic Church, Flandreau, 1917 [8/8/2006]

Midway Lutheran Church, 5 miles north, 9.5 miles west of Flandreau, 1925 [8/9/2006]

OGLALA LAKOTA COUNTY (formerly Shannon County)

Holy Cross Episcopal Church, Pine Ridge, 1884 [9/6/2005]

Saint Andrew's Episcopal Church, Wakpamani Lake, 1884 [6/14/2010]

Saint John's Episcopal Church, 8 miles north of Oglala, 1888 (originally Church of the Holy Fellowship at Holy Cross Mission, Pine Ridge) [9/9/2010]

Interior, Saint John's Episcopal Church

Our Lady of Good Council Church, 11 miles north of Oglala, 1909 [9/4/2005]

Interior, Our Lady of Good Council Church

Saint Julia's Episcopal Church, Porcupine, 1910 [9/9/2010]

Saint Agnes Catholic Church, Manderson, 1911 [9/9/2010]

Saint Joseph's Catholic Church, Cuny Table, 1925 (built as a school) [9/9/2010]

Sacred Heart Catholic Church, Pine Ridge, 1927, closed as a church after 1970 [9/9/2010]

Mary Magdelen Church, Cuny Table, date unknown (moved from Sharps Corner in 1986) [9/5/2010]

Saint Alban's Episcopal Church, 5 miles north of Porcupine, date unknown [9/9/2010]

Church of Saint Stephen (Catholic), Kyle, 1911 [9/9/2010]

Saint Peter's Catholic Church, 8 miles north of Manderson, date unknown [9/9/2010]

Church of God, Wounded Knee, date unknown [9/9/2010]

Emmanuel Episcopal Church, Rapid City, 1888 [8/2/2005]

United Church of Christ, Keystone, 1896 [9/11/2010]

The Little White Church, Hill City, 1890 [7/5/2007]

Immaculate Conception Catholic Church, Rapid City, 1909 [8/2/2005]

Interior, Immaculate Conception Catholic Church

Faith Temple, Rapid City, 1914 (Congregational until 1982) [8/2/2005]

Folsom Baptist Church, 11 miles south of Farmingdale, 1917 [7/8/2007]

PERKINS COUNTY

Duck Creek Lutheran Church, 5.5 miles west, 2 miles south of Lodgepole, 1900 [7/28/2007]

Lemmon Baptist Church, Lemmon, 1908 [7/28/2007]

Homme Lutheran Church, Prairie City, 1911 (built in Maltby Township, moved 1960s) [6/19/2010]

Lodgepole Lutheran Church, Lodgepole, 1917 (Union Church until 1965) [7/28/2007]

Little White Church, Bison, 1918 [7/28/2007]

Little White Church from a distance

Saint James Catholic Church, 15 miles south, 4.5 miles west of Bison, 1920 [7/28/2007]

Rosebud Lutheran Church, 10 miles west of Shadehill, 1921 [7/28/2007]

Immanuel Lutheran Church, Zeona, 1927 [7/29/2007]

POTTER COUNTY

Unknown church, Hoven, 1905 (originally Saint Anthony's Catholic in Selby, moved 1972) [5/19/2008]

Seventh Day Adventist Church, Tolstoy, ca. 1910, enlarged in 1948 [5/19/2008]

United Methodist Church, Tolstoy, date unknown (bought from Baptists in 1912) [5/19/2008]

Saint Anthony of Padua Catholic Church, Hoven, 1921 [5/25/2010]

United Methodist Church, Gettysburg, 1927 [5/19/2008]

ROBERTS COUNTY

Ascension Presbyterian Church, 5 miles south, 4 miles west of Peever, 1874 [7/17/2007]

Saint Mary's Episcopal Church, 1 mile north, 5 miles west of Peever, 1882 [7/17/2007]

Augustana Lutheran Church, White Rock, 1891, closed 1997 [7/17/2007]

Zoar Lutheran Church, 8 miles west of Peever, 1893 [7/17/2007]

Lake Traverse Presbyterian Church, 5 miles north of Browns Valley, 1895 [7/17/2007]

Hope Lutheran Church, Summit, 1898 [7/17/2007]

Summit Bible Church, Summit, 1898 (formerly Baptist) [7/17/2007]

Walla Lutheran Church, New Effington, 1902 [5/27/2010]

Free Methodist Church, Ortley, 1906 [7/17/2007]

Bethania-Trondhjem Lutheran Church, 6 miles south, 1.5 miles west of Rosholt, 1900 [5/27/2010]

Zion Lutheran Church, 4 miles north, 2 miles east of Claire City, 1902 [7/18/2007]

Ortley Free Lutheran Church, Ortley, 1908 (formerly Zion Lutheran) [7/17/2007]

Emanuel Lutheran Church, Sisseton, 1916 (moved 1948) [7/18/2007]

First Presbyterian Church, Sisseton, 1922 [7/18/2007]

Sacred Heart Catholic Church, New Effington, 1913 [5/22/2009]

Unknown church, 8 miles north, 2 miles west of Browns Valley, Minnesota, date unknown [7/17/2007]

SANBORN COUNTY

First Methodist Church, Artesian, 1886 (originally Diana Methodist Episcopal Church), north side addition 1965 [5/23/2012]

United Church of Christ, Letcher, 1903 (formerly Congregational) [8/10/2006]

Bethany Lutheran Church, Woonsocket, 1910 (built in Silver Creek Township, moved in 1934) [8/10/2006]

Saint Wilfrid's Catholic Church, Woonsocket, 1920 [6/17/2010]

Saint Scholastica Catholic Church, Letcher, 1924 [8/10/2006]

Trinity Lutheran Church, 3 miles east of Storla, 1925 [6/17/2010]

SPINK COUNTY

United Methodist Church, Ashton, 1883 [8/14/2007]

Redeemer Lutheran Church, Doland, 1885 [6/17/2010]

First Congregational Church, Turton, 1893 [6/17/2010]

Saint John the Baptist Catholic Church, Conde, 1905 [7/16/2009]

Brentford Congregational Church, Brentford, 1906 [6/17/2010]

First Congregational United Church of Christ, Redfield, 1908 [8/14/2007]

Saint Bernard's Catholic Church, Redfield, 1908 [8/14/2007]

Salem United Church of Christ, Tulare, 1911 [8/13/2007]

Saint Joseph's Catholic Church, Turton, 1919 [8/14/2007]

Bethany Lutheran Church, 4 miles north, 6.5 miles east of Mellette, 1920 [5/25/2012]

Saint Ann's Catholic Church, Frankfort, 1922 [6/18/2010]

United Methodist Church, Doland, 1922 [8/12/2007]

Trinity Lutheran Church, 1 mile south, 5 miles west of Mansfield, 1926 [8/17/2007]

STANLEY COUNTY

Congregational United Church of Christ, Fort Pierre, 1909 [8/18/2005]

Little Brown Church on the Prairie (United Methodist), 2 miles west of Hayes, 1923 [8/18/2005]

Grace Lutheran Church, Hayes, date unknown [6/18/2010]

SULLY COUNTY

Saint Pius X Catholic Church, Onida, 1906 [5/25/2010]

Saint John's Lutheran Church, Agar, 1910 [5/20/2008]

First Presbyterian Church, Onida, date unknown [5/20/2008]

TODD COUNTY

Episcopal Mission Church of Jesus, Rosebud, 1875 [5/17/2005]

Rosebud Lutheran Church, Rosebud, 1905 (Saint Bridget Catholic until 2002) [6/15/2010]

Okreek Episcopal Church, Okreek, 1914 [6/15/2010]

Saint Charles Borromeo Catholic Church, Saint Francis, 1922 [8/16/2005]

Saint Patrick's Catholic Church, Spring Creek, 1922 [9/3/2005]

Saint Agnes Catholic Church, Parmelee, 1927, replaced in 1974 [8/16/2005]

Sacred Heart Catholic Church, 10 miles west of Parmelee, date unknown (moved to current location 1940s), closed 2003 [8/20/2005]

Holy Innocents Episcopal Church, 1 mile west of Parmelee, date unknown [9/3/2005]

Saint Isidore Catholic Church, Colome, 1910 [6/6/2006]

Ascension Chapel, Millboro, 1911 (built as Star Prairie Sunday School) [6/5/2006]

United Methodist Church, Colome, 1911, became Odd Fellows Lodge in 1926 [6/6/2006]

Indian Gospel Chapel, Winner, 1912 (formerly Methodist) [6/5/2006]

Zion Lutheran Church, Hamill, 1914 [6/6/2006]

Paxton Methodist Church, 1 mile east of Winner, 1915 (moved from Paxton), now in Tripp County Museum [6/5/2006]

Lakeview Methodist Church, 1 mile east of Winner, 1917 (built near Dog Ear Lake), closed 1974, now in Tripp County Museum [6/5/2006]

Saint Boniface Catholic Church, 1 mile north, 0.5 mile east of Clearfield, 1920 [6/15/2010]

Zion Lutheran Church, Colome, 1924 [6/6/2006]

United Church of Christ, Millboro, 1924 [6/15/2010]

United Methodist Church, Colome, 1926 [6/6/2006]

Saint John Evangelical Lutheran Church, Witten, 1928 [6/5/2006]

Saint John the Baptist Catholic Church, Witten, date unknown, abandoned 1997 [6/5/2006]

TURNER COUNTY

First English Lutheran Church, Parker, 1882 [7/15/2009]

First Baptist Church, Centerville, 1884 [5/23/2012]

Harmony Presbyterian Church, Hurley, 1885, additions 1916, 1970, 1889 (bell) [6/22/2006]

First English Lutheran Church, Centerville, 1885 [6/17/2010]

United Methodist Church, Hurley, 1890 [5/23/2012]

First Presbyterian Church, Parker, 1891 [6/22/2006]

Federated United Church of Christ, Centerville, 1891 [6/23/2006]

Viborg United Methodist Church, Viborg, 1894 [7/15/2009]

Immanuel Lutheran Church, 4 miles west, 2 miles south of Centerville, 1898 [9/27/2014]

First Reformed Church, Monroe, 1898, remodeled 1950s, tall steeple removed [6/23/2006]

Salem Free Lutheran Church, Turkey Ridge, 1905 [6/23/2006]

Scandia Lutheran Church, Centerville, 1910, enlarged 1957 [7/15/2009]

Saint Christina Catholic Church, Parker, 1911 [7/15/2009]

Our Savior Lutheran Church, Viborg, 1911 [7/15/2009]

Bethany Lutheran Church, Hurley, 1912 [7/15/2009]

Bethany Lutheran Church, Viborg, 1915 [7/15/2009]

First Baptist Church, Viborg, 1917 [7/15/2009]

Bethel Christian Reformed Church, Marion, 1929 [6/17/2010]

Emmanuel Presbyterian Church, Marion, 1925 [6/22/2006]

Zion Lutheran Church, Hurley, date unknown (moved from southwest of Freeman in 1961) [7/15/2009]

Grace Lutheran Church, Parker, date unknown (moved from Maple Grove ca. 1947) [5/23/2012]

UNION COUNTY

Old Big Springs Baptist Church, Big Springs, 1874 [6/7/2006]

Saint Peter's Catholic Church, Jefferson, 1891 [7/14/2009]

Interior, Saint Peter's Catholic Church

Big Springs Baptist Church, Big Springs, 1898 [6/7/2006]

Stavanger Lutheran Church, North Sioux City, 1902 (built 13 miles south of Kimball), restored 1993, now in Adams Nature Center [6/7/2006]

Alcester Baptist Church, Alcester, 1902 [6/8/2006]

Elk Point Baptist Church, Elk Point, ca. 1905 (originally Methodist) [7/14/2009]

Roseni Lutheran Church, 5 miles north, 2 miles east of Spink, 1912 [6/7/2006]

United Brethren Church (aka Pleasant Hill Chapel), 1.5 miles north, 3 miles east of Pleasant Hill, 1905, on National Register of Historic Places [6/7/2006]

Saint Paul's Lutheran Church, 5 miles north, 1 mile east of Elk Point, 1922 [7/14/2009]

Union Creek Lutheran Church, 3.5 miles south, 1 mile east of Big Springs, 1926 [6/7/2006]

WALWORTH COUNTY

Bethany Lutheran Church, 3 miles north, 7 miles east of Glenham, 1885 [5/20/2008]

Lowry Pilgrim Community Church, Lowry, 1901 [5/20/2008]

United Methodist Church, Mobridge, 1908 (originally Trinity Lutheran Church) [5/26/2010]

Grace Congregational Church, Mobridge, 1910 (originally Saint Joseph's Catholic) [5/25/2012]

Saint James Episcopal Church, Mobridge, 1919 [5/20/2008]

Seventh Day Adventist Church, Mobridge, 1925 [5/25/2012]

Saint Jacobi Evangelical Lutheran Church, Glenham, 1926 [5/20/2008]

Zion Lutheran Church, Akaska, 1929 [5/20/2008]

First Baptist Church, Mobridge, 1929 [5/19/2008]

United Church of Christ, Java, date unknown (Lutheran until 1959) [5/19/2008]

YANKTON COUNTY

Old Vangen Lutheran Church, 1 mile east of Mission Hill, 1869 (oldest standing church in South Dakota) [5/23/2012]

Antioch Baptist Church, Yankton, 1879 [5/22/2006]

Christ Church Episcopal, Yankton, 1882 (oldest Episcopal church in the state) [5/24/2006]

Saint John the Baptist Catholic Church, 6 miles east of Tabor, 1884 [5/25/2006]

Interior, Saint John the Baptist Catholic Church

African Methodist Episcopal Church, Yankton, 1885 [5/25/2006]

Gayville Methodist Church, Gayville, 1891 [7/14/2009]

Saint Columba Catholic Church, 1 mile north of Mayfield, 1902 [6/16/2010]

Kingsway Lutheran Church, Yankton, 1902 [5/22/2012]

United Church of Christ, Yankton, 1904 [5/25/2006]

Saint Agnes Catholic Church, 10 miles north, 1 mile west of Yankton, 1908 [5/25/2006]

Faith United Lutheran Church, 3 miles north, 2 miles west of Volin, 1916 (formerly Zion Lutheran) [6/16/2010]

Harvest Independent Baptist Church, Mission Hill, 1917 [5/25/2006]

Vangen Lutheran Church (newer), Mission Hill, 1917 [5/25/2006]

Saint John the Baptist Catholic Church, Lesterville, 1919 [6/16/2010]

Faith Alive Church, Yankton, 1922 (originally United Brethren of Christ) [5/25/2006]

ZIEBACH COUNTY

Church of Saint Joseph (Catholic), Cherry Creek, 1894 [6/18/2010]

United Church of Christ, Dupree, 1917 [5/26/2012]

Saint Luke's Catholic Church, Thunder Butte, 1913 [8/19/2005]

Sacred Heart Catholic Church, Dupree, 1913, now a museum 5/26/2012]

Index